The Journalist's Primer

A No-Nonsense Guide to Getting and Reporting the News

By Mark Hanebutt

University of Central Oklahoma

Kendall Hunt
publishing company

Cover image © Adam Gault

Kendall Hunt
publishing company

www.kendallhunt.com
Send all inquiries to:
4050 Westmark Drive
Dubuque, IA 52004-1840

Printed in the United States of America
10 9 8 7 6 5 4 3

For my parents —
who taught me the value of reading the newspaper.

Contents

Acknowledgements

I appreciate the contributions of Dick Pryor, deputy director and managing editor of the Oklahoma Educational Television Authority (OETA), and University of Central Oklahoma professors Terry M. Clark, Bill Hickman, David Nelson, and Mark Zimmerman. Their assistance in creating this text has been invaluable.

I also wish to acknowledge Adam Gault for the cover design and Kendall Hunt Publishing Company representative Jaafar Gassid and project coordinator Thalia Cutsforth for their assistance.

Thank you.

Introduction

No one who has been in the classroom for any length of time can be under the illusion that students will wade unthreatened through a 500-page textbook. Consequently, after searching unsuccessfully for twenty-five years for a text that would not double as a doorstop, I've given up and written my own.

If you're a teacher looking for a guidebook to take the student briefly and chronologically through the basic theory and practice of news reporting, perhaps you will find this useful. If you want the full encyclopedia of journalism, look elsewhere.

This book is designed to help teachers with a background in journalism move the student through a 15-week semester focusing on the basics. It does not include a DVD, lesson plans, practice tests, teachers' guides, or other aids, though it does offer a suggested exercise for students at the back of each chapter. It doesn't have comments from youthful reporters and there are no long treatises on the world of emerging media — whatever that is. This is not about technology. This is about fundamentals, whatever the method of delivering them. Technology changes, fundamentals do not. And if anyone — even laypeople — understand anything about the news media today, it's that reporters don't always understand the fundamentals necessary to maintain a free press and an enlightened democracy.

This book was written by a journalist who once worked at a big city daily, then went off to teach college because he thought he could do some good. In the meantime, things changed, and now he can't stand to watch the evening news for all the personality, self-promotion, commentary, innuendo, agenda setting, trivia, and unanswered questions.

Hence, I've decided to explain why we have a free press, what news is, and how to go out and get it and present it without getting in the way — in other words, the basics.

Mark Hanebutt
January 1, 2012
Oklahoma City

CHAPTER 1

Theory of the Press in a Democratic Society

• Humans and the Quest for Truth •

To understand why and how the Press — the generic term for all news media — works, one must first understand how people work — that is, one must understand the characteristics of human beings. (Bear with me. This is deep, but not as deep as accounting.) People, of course, have many different characteristics. We love, we hate, we can be greedy and self-centered while at other times generous and selfless. We're complicated. Our characteristics as humans, and our experience dealing with those characteristics, give rise to the values we hold. For example, because we are fearful (and often hurt when not treated fairly) and curious (and often benefit from knowing), we value justice and truth. Professions exist to address some of these basic values. The law gives us justice, medicine provides us with health, and journalism and education exist to help us find truth. So the Press, in a very real sense, is merely a means to an end — that is, it exists to help us achieve something we value — truth.

And therein lies the problem. Not everyone agrees on just what truth is. That's because truth is usually viewed as subjective. One man's truth is another man's lie. Look at all the different religions in the world, all the different concepts of God. Look at the different views on politics. We have these different views because we have different life experiences, different physical characteristics, different strengths, weaknesses, different parents, education, cultures, etc. We are all individuals. And as individuals, we are a composite of a bunch of stuff.

Since no one knows absolute truth, what philosophers often call *Big T*, no one can be certain his view of truth is correct. As humans, we are limited in our ability to know truth, and can never know absolute truth because we know only through our five senses — our ability to taste, touch, smell, see, and hear — and our emotions and our ability to reason — our intellect.

This does not stop us, of course, from being certain in our view of truth. In fact, some of us are so certain that we are willing to go to war over it on occasion. Historically, religion — man's ultimate view of truth — has been at the heart of many conflicts. Remember the Crusades, the Spanish Inquisition? Since we can never know absolute truth, this should give us pause and make us tolerant of other views, but it doesn't. Unfortunately, that's another human characteristic.

To get at the heart of truth, philosophers and other thinkers throughout history have struggled to identify its universal characteristics. Ancient man, with his oral history, thought it was whatever could be remembered. Obviously, it was believed, if an experience were important enough to be remembered, it must be true. Plato said truth resided in the mind as a product of rationality and intellect. Nothing had meaning until conceptualized in the mind. A chair wasn't a chair until someone thought it up in his head. During the Medieval period, when the Church grew in strength, truth was whatever the priest or king said it was. It represented a top-to-bottom vision of truth, which suited the power hierarchy.

A number of important world events from the fourteenth through eighteenth centuries — including the cultural rebirth of The Renaissance, the spread of world markets and trade during The Age of Discovery, the spread of the scientific revolution during The Enlightenment, the spread of critical thought during The Protestant Reformation, and the rise of humanism — helped bring about new ideas of truth. All of these movements were aided by the invention of the movable-type printing press by Johannes Gutenberg about 1450. Arguably the most important invention in human history, the printing press spread literacy and education throughout the world by making information cheap and affordable to the masses and brought about the birth of the modern newspaper. In a sense it ushered in the age of shared knowledge and widespread critical thought. In short, people began to think for themselves. As a result, it also was seen as a threat to those hierarchies in power at the time and, indeed, eventually helped bring about their fall.

As a result of these changes, two new philosophies of truth emerged, primarily in the seventeenth and eighteenth centuries, that became the philosophical basis for modern democracies today and, in turn, the modern libertarian Press. The United States, the first modern democracy, was the first to embrace these philosophies as the basis for its new government after the American Revolution. It's the adoption of these philosophies as the basis of government that makes America unique in world history. It is important to understand both of these in order to understand the American democracy and the American Press and how the two are linked.

• John Milton and a New Look at Truth •

The first philosophy of truth emerged from John Milton's theory laid down in his treatise *Areopagitica* — probably history's most eloquent defense of freedom of expression and press. In part, he wrote:

> *[T]hough all the winds of doctrine were let loose to play on the earth, so Truth be in the field, we do injuriously, by licensing and prohibiting, to misdoubt her strength. Let her and Falsehood grapple; who ever knew Truth put to the worse, in a free and open encounter?*

It was published in 1644 in opposition to licensing and censorship at a time when licensing and censorship by the authorities was the norm. Milton's theory grew out of Christian theology as expressed in John 8:32 (*...the truth will set you free.*) His belief was that since God is truth and that since God made man in his own image and wanted man to know him, he gave man the ability to know truth. Truth was not, therefore, revealed through official doctrine by a select line of authority of kings and priests — the view of the day — but to all mankind through inquiry and debate and reason — characteristics God gave man. Furthermore, Milton argued, if God is truth and God is all-powerful, truth will win out in any open debate. Therefore, he said we should put all ideas out for debate, thought, and inquiry. We should put the lie up against the truth since truth will win in the end.

The ultimate evil, in Milton's view, is censorship, since censorship allows some to prevent others from seeing those conflicting ideas and finding the truth for themselves. Those who censor, in essence, are saying they have the divine gift to discern truth while others do not and cannot be trusted with the task of finding the truth on their own.

This new philosophy urging individual inquiry in theory made every man intellectually equal to every other man and gave each the right to seek truth on his own. It, again in theory, gave the common man as much power as the nobleman and priest, and empowered men to govern without benefit of king or spiritual leader to dictate official truth. It was an idea that encouraged independent thought and threatened the absolute power of monarchies and theocracies and helped usher in democracy.

We see Milton's theory at work everywhere in our government. We probably see it best in our judicial system. Each lawyer gets up in open court before the public and argues to the jury that his client's story is the correct version of the truth. The jury watches the fight — the grappling — and decides where the truth lies by its verdict. Our Congress debates laws in the open chambers of the Senate and House of Representatives and before the Press and public in the gallery and then votes on where they think the truth lies in the matter. We, the people, listen to the debates of candidates for office and then cast our votes, deciding who has the better version of the truth. Milton's view then relies heavily not only on individual discernment of truth, but also, when it comes to government, on public consensus.

• The Enlightenment — Founding Principle of a New Kind of Country •

The second philosophy one must understand came out of The Enlightenment theory of truth. As we noted earlier, the problem with truth, according to most views, is that it is subjective. The Enlightenment brought a different view of truth. Known as The Scientific Revolution or The Age of Reason, The Enlightenment looked at truth objectively, scientifically. Truth wasn't subject to the whim of individual interpretation or tradition. It was based on fact and evidence. It could be proven and replicated. It was unchanging since facts are unchanging. It was scientific. It was rational.

The Enlightenment began after the Dark Ages — a time of ignorance and fear and mysticism — ended and man began to use his rational abilities. Belief in natural law evolved. Empiricism — the view that knowledge comes through experience and experimentation — grew in importance.

The Enlightenment and the move toward empirical thought gave rise to what we call the Scientific Method, a kind of inquiry that all students learn today in school. Every time a student writes a term paper or engages in a science experiment, that student is using the Scientific Method. One starts with a hypothesis and then gathers evidence to prove or disprove it. It is this method that we use to discover new things about our world and universe. Objective, provable, unchanging fact then is at the heart of truthful inquiry under The Enlightenment.

This rationality extended not only to scientific thought — which led to experimental science and all the scientific discoveries we have realized since, but also to politics and social issues — which figured significantly before and during the American Revolution. Enlightenment thinkers included, among others, Voltaire (1694-1766) and Jean-Jacques Rousseau (1712-1788) and John Locke (1632-1704).

Locke and others extended this rational philosophy to government in a doctrine known as The Social Contract Theory — the view that government is a social contract between citizens and their leaders based on the will and needs of the governed. Social Contract theorists believe man has natural freedoms, but that a rational person gives up some of his natural freedoms in exchange for the benefits and protections of political order. Therefore, government is established to protect life, liberty, and property — what Locke called inalienable rights. (Thomas Jefferson would later call them life, liberty, and the pursuit of happiness in the Declaration of Independence.) Locke believed that public welfare makes government necessary and that citizens have obligations in pursuit of that government. Furthermore, Locke believed that any time government subverts that purpose, it should be deposed. This philosophy was at the heart of the American and French Revolutions.

Again, as with Milton, we see The Enlightenment and the emerging Social Contract theory as essential ingredients in American democracy. We also see them in the way the Press works, or is supposed to work. While Milton argued that man should be free to decide the truth for himself, and consequently, when it came to political matters, to decide collectively with his fellow citizens; Locke argued that man should pursue this individual inquiry of truth — not on the basis of personal whim or mysticism — but on the basis of rational, empirical thought which should lead to the knowledge necessary to maintain that social contract between man and his government.

In this combination of philosophies — Milton and Locke — we see the way western democracies and the western Press are supposed to function. We reach truth individually and collectively after we have researched the facts and reached a dispassionate, objective conclusion. We are not supposed to choose leaders, pass laws, or convict those in court on the basis of emotional appeal and personal bias, but on the basis of political records and political positions, the reasonableness of any proposed law, and the facts of each individual case. In this way we discover truth and maintain our natural freedoms and the government that protects them.

• The Press — Linchpin of Democracy •

By now you should be able to anticipate where the Press fits into this new system. It is the linchpin that holds it together. At the heart of any system of truth that relies on individual freedom, corporate consensus, and objective information must be a method that enables the three to come together. We must be able to get and share credible, unbiased, factual information to find the truth in any matter. No jury could reach an accurate verdict on the guilt or innocence of an accused without being presented the facts of the case. So too, no citizen can reach a credible decision about the future of his life or those of his countrymen without receiving accurate, objective, complete information about the events of the day. Given its ability to gather, print, and distribute information cheaply, the Press became the most effective means to achieve this end in the new democracy.

Even the Founding Fathers understood the essential nature of this task given the philosophical basis of the new nation, and consequently, the importance of the Press. They understood that knowledge and open thought and discussion of ideas were necessary means to finding the truth and envisioned a Press that would challenge the dogma of the status quo, question authority, foster debate, and demand answers from those in power. They saw the need for a Press that would promote change, help right wrongs, and play an active role in helping people find truth.

And they were vocal about it —

> *"A popular Government, without popular information, or the means of acquiring it, is but a Prologue to a Farce or a Tragedy; or, perhaps both. Knowledge will forever govern ignorance: And a people who mean to be their own Governors must arm themselves with the power which knowledge gives." — James Madison*

> *"Were it left to me to decide whether we should have a government without newspapers, or newspapers without a government, I should not hesitate a moment but to prefer the latter." — Thomas Jefferson*

If commerce was the lifeblood of the nation, the Founders understood the Press was its nervous system.

Two other philosophies deserve mentioning to help us understand how the Press should work today. They are Pragmatism and Postmodernism. Both are important to modern journalism because they add other dimensions to truth that should be considered when attempting to provide the citizen with adequate information.

Pragmatists discard The Enlightenment approach by noting that truth is not determined by one objective view and is instead defined as that which is probable. Truth depends on who is doing the investigating. Indeed, the pragmatist would argue that truth by definition is an individual interpretation of facts and of perception, not the facts themselves. And truth isn't truth until that individual interpretation is involved, bringing with it all the characteristics human beings possess to help them interpret. Under this view, truth is not universal but individual and therefore relative. What is real cannot be found unless one takes into consideration historical, social, cultural, and psychological contexts.

From a journalistic standpoint, this presents a problem. Under traditional notions of Enlightenment-based journalism, truth and opinion are strictly separated. The benefit of this is that when someone is given the facts, they can interpret them for themselves. On the other hand, when they are reading someone else's interpretation of facts, they are denied that chance. The facts, if you will, have become polluted with opinion and the perceptions of others. It is for that reason that credible journalism attempts to keep fact and opinion separate by including only facts in news stories and opinion in editorials and labeled opinion pieces. Yet the pragmatist argues this, too, is impossible, noting the facts observed and presented are selected by individuals with individual perceptions and biases.

Postmodernism asserts that meaning is not attainable apart from context. The context of a message includes the source of the information, who is delivering the information and who is receiving it. It includes facts, opinions, everything. Postmodernists argue that all of this must be considered before we can make sense of any message.

For example, to fully understand a story on gun control we must know who is providing us with the information. It matters whether the information is coming from, say, the National Rifle Association or a gun control lobbying group. The facts may be the same, but the message may change given which facts are included, which are excluded, and how the facts used are emphasized, organized, and delivered.

Postmodernists argue that apart from context, meaning, and therefore truth, cannot exist. Think of a story coming out of the Middle East. Then think how the reality of that story changes depending on who delivers the message and who receives it. Fox News, NBC, and Al Jazeera may report the same story but in different ways. The meaning can and does change even if we are still just reporting Enlightenment-based facts. So it's not just the facts, but also the context of the facts.

Conscientious journalists wrestle with these dilemmas and attempt to accommodate these different concepts of truth by being as objective as possible, by quoting people with different views and by providing a broad context of the facts. Consequently, in today's world, journalists should be careful to consider Milton and Locke as well as pragmatic and postmodern views. Even then, attaining something akin to truth is difficult.

• Exercise •

Research and write reports on John Milton's *Areopagitica* and his views on free expression and John Locke's views on representative government under The Social Contract Theory. Deliver orally and discuss.

• The Importance of Credibility •

In most journalism textbooks, the chapter on ethics comes last — as if to say, if we have time, we'll go over it, if not, no big deal. Given the state of American journalism, most professors apparently don't have time to cover it. (I've kept the chapters short in this book so you'll have plenty of time to make it through law.)

The reality is that ethics, next to understanding the purpose of the Press in a democratic society (Chapter 1), is more important than anything else that follows in this book. In short, it doesn't matter how well you write a story, if you have no credibility, if you betray the fundamental purpose of the Press and the people it serves, you're no more useful than the little boy who cried wolf one too many times.

The goal of the journalist is to help people find truth. The primary purpose of journalism is not to help publishers amass a fortune, improve broadcast ratings, win awards, or make yourself famous. Consequently, how you go about getting the news is as important as the task of news reporting itself, and a journalist must understand that first — not last.

• The Deteriorating Reputation of the Press •

Unfortunately, in terms of fairness, accuracy, and believability, the reputation of the Press has eroded significantly during the past three decades, according to The Pew Research Center's Project for Excellence in Journalism. In the 1980s more people thought the news media was accurate than did not. Today, the numbers are reversed. Citizens think the news media favors one political side over another and that it's lost its independence to powerful people.

This does not bode well for the industry or the democracy. One of the fundamental purposes of the Press is to serve as watchdog of government, to make sure that those in power do not abuse their authority. After all, if a people truly wish to be in charge of their government, they must know what it's doing. But what happens if the dog barks when something's wrong and no one listens? What happens when we believe the politicians with the power instead of the media that checks them?

Changes in the news industry as well as our society are to blame for this erosion of confidence. In the 1960s TV anchors presented the news much the way newspaper people did. An attempt was made to be objective, and on-air delivery was mostly straightforward and sober, focusing on government and public issues.

But in an effort to make more money, particularly after the advent of cable television and the increased competition it brought, the race was on to attract viewers by making the news more personable and entertaining. The era of *happy talk* journalism was born. Anchors no longer attempted to provide a droll litany of the day's news. Now they bantered with one another on air and proceeded to interject their own personality and opinion into the newscast with a raised eyebrow or an idle off-the-cuff comment. The result was a subjective presentation of the news, if not in fact, in manner.

Too, the news suddenly wasn't about boring government meetings, bills, and budgets, despite the fact such things might affect millions of people. Instead, it was about anything that would shock, entertain, or pander. In effect, the news became just another show to attract viewers, increase ratings, and make money.

The problem with this, of course, is that it hurt credibility. It's difficult to argue or take sides with facts, but when you start to offer opinions, you might be wrong. And you invite disagreement. And how important are you when you present cute stories about dogs in the snow? Citizens can dismiss as irrelevant news and newspeople that entertain only. No longer are you the wise sage; now you're the community clown.

Cable TV also provided us with another problem — 24-hour news. Before cable, reporters had all day to gather information, check it, write it, re-check it, and present it. Now reporters had to find news and present it every hour. This increased speed meant less time to check facts or report in context. Credibility took another hit.

To add to the problem, the increased competition from additional television channels meant more media outlets had to share less profit. Reporters became an expensive luxury. Managers found it was cheaper to present fluff stories that could be churned out quickly for the new 24-hour news format than hard news that required expensive, experienced reporters, time, and money. As the number of reporters dwindled, so did the quality of the news that was presented, not only on TV, but in newspapers as well. Less money also meant the size of newspapers shrank, which meant there were fewer and shorter stories to read.

Instead of news, the media turned to marketable personalities who could host talk shows. Suddenly, one news topic could fill hours of airtime. The news now was a series of various people giving their opinions on what the news meant. Of course, anyone was free to disagree with them. The focus was about opinion and how loudly and quickly you could talk.

Enter the Internet. Suddenly you didn't even need to buy a newspaper or turn on the radio or TV. Now you could get the news every second of the day just by going online — despite the fact most online sites didn't have their own reporters and were getting the news from traditional media. As a result, ad revenue for the legacy media — newspapers, magazines, radio, and TV, which paid for the reporters — began to fall as people turned to the free news. News staffs, in turn, dwindled. Newspapers closed. Yes, people could now get their news for free, but what would happen when the reporters could no longer find work? Where would the news come from then?

Of course, now that anyone could get on the web, anyone could report the news, even if they didn't know how. Consequently, the news managers found a new source of news, even if it was wrong. Citizens could Tweet or post on Facebook or send it in to their local media. Suddenly, everyone was a reporter. Except, just as suddenly it became even more difficult to tell who was credible and who was not.

Nevertheless, now everyone was talking at once. It was Milton's theory of the marketplace of ideas realized at last. It was the democratization of information. And it was a Tower of Babel.

The result has been a crisis of confidence in the news. Things sped up. Attention spans shrank. Difficult or complex issues were dismissed out of hand. Facts became less important than opinions. No one wanted to listen to the hard questions and the complex answers. We wanted it fast and simple and easy — and entertaining, even if it wasn't.

And now that everyone was talking — and talking about everything — who was listening? And which conversation were they listening to? The media had become fragmented, and so too, the messages. Were there enough people listening to the same topic long enough to reach a consensus on anything of importance? And who was right? Was the news bringing us together, or was it splitting us apart because now we were no longer looking for facts — just those we agreed with, even if they were wrong?

• From the Age of Reason to the Age of Aesthetics •

This crisis wasn't entirely the fault of the Press. A lot of this had to do with the way people now thought and the way society was teaching people to think — or perhaps we should say, feel.

The primary discourse became advertising, not news, and advertisers found they could persuade easier with emotion than logic. Advertising encouraged us to make decisions on the basis of how we felt or how pleasant something appeared, not how reasonable or factual it was. Consequently, we began to choose leaders the same way we choose cars — because we thought they looked good, not because they had the right policies or, in the case of cars, the right gas mileage.

We left the Age of Reason and entered the Age of Aesthetics. So who needed a Press that focused on facts? We wanted to feel good, and we wanted a Press that would accommodate us. Had the American people themselves lost sight of the reasons for the Press — to give us information and challenge the status quo, concepts at the heart of the American Revolution?

• Changes in the Law •

Changes in the law also played a part in this crisis of confidence. In exchange for broadcast licenses, the government had required broadcasters to operate in the public interest since they were transmitting over public airwaves. But the Federal Communications Commission, responsible for regulating the industry, eliminated two rules that arguably promoted credibility.

The Fairness Doctrine required that all broadcasters had to provide coverage of important public issues in their communities and that all significant viewpoints on the issues had to be aired. Also, personal attack rules had required that if broadcasters aired a personal attack on an individual or group, they had to notify those attacked and offer free time for a reply. The same rule applied to editorials. But the Court ordered the rules repealed on First Amendment grounds.

• A Flawed Philosophy and The Social Responsibility Theory •

The credibility problem of the Press then is multi-layered. It was born out of greed that placed profit above objective news reporting; it came from technology that changed the way we presented the news; and it came from the people themselves who perhaps forgot that finding truth and maintaining a democracy required individual responsibility to stay informed and that knowledge didn't always come quickly or simply or easily, or because of the way we felt.

15

The news media, of course, has not always been a paragon of objectivity. In the early days of the republic, newspapers were rife with commentary and innuendo. The Founders expected a free-for-all of ideas and opinions and facts mixed together. That different political parties had their own newspaper mouthpieces was expected. Even today, some suggest that the pursuit of objectivity is folly since all humans are inherently subjective. And commentary and debate are equally useful, they argue. People, they point out, are not always rational and don't always make rational decisions, despite the Enlightenment principles.

In fact, the libertarian theory discussed in Chapter 1, which focused on the rationality of man and the idea that he would be responsible and enlightened enough to pursue information on his own, has indeed in some ways been discredited. We have learned that we are not always rational and truth is subject to individual whim.

A group called the Hutchins Commission, believing citizens needed help in their quest for truth, attempted to define the goals of the Press in a doctrine in the 1940s that became known as The Social Responsibility Theory. Recognizing that people were often lazy and not always civically engaged, the media, it was believed, should pursue five functions on their behalf, including:

1. Providing a truthful and comprehensive account of the day's news in context.
2. Providing a public forum for the discussion of important ideas.
3. Providing an accurate picture of society's various constituencies.
4. Giving a clear picture of society's goals and values.
5. Providing citizens with access to the day's intelligence.

The effort was viewed as too paternalistic, interfering with citizens' duty to stay informed, and largely has been abandoned by journalists.

Still, the need for credible, detailed, factual information is more important than ever in this highly technical age — whether it's our individual responsibility to find it or the media's. And if we are inclined to find truth, we are more likely to find it if we pursue objectivity than if we abandon it. Too, the credibility of the Press is likely to increase if it presents accurate, objective information. Unfortunately, as the world has become increasingly complex, the media messages have become increasingly less so, making the goal even more elusive.

• Building Trust by Making Ethical Decisions •

Faced with the current public suspicion of the media, journalists today who wish to be believed have their work cut out for them. Consequently, the need for solid ethical reasoning and decision-making is more important than ever. This doesn't mean pandering to the public, but it does mean understanding clearly what your purpose is and acting in such a way that others understand it, too. And so, first and foremost, the credible journalist must understand those principles and purposes laid down in the first chapter. The next step is to make ethical decisions that support those principles.

People often have a difficult time understanding ethics and get it confused with morality or law. All are useful, but all are different. Law exists to provide order; it is the basis of civilization. Morality is where we get our concepts of right and wrong, good and bad. These ideas are usually adopted from the realm of religion. (Don't confuse law and morality. The Nazis passed laws for the orderly murder of six million Jews. Laws can be good or bad. They're purpose is order.)

Ethics begins where morality leaves off. It is the rational choice between competing moral positions or ideals. It's about making choices and the reasons and justification for those choices.

For example, let's say you're a moral person. You believe that you shouldn't lie, but you also believe you should not allow others to be hurt. You learn that if you misrepresent yourself, you might get information that will show the mayor is embezzling city funds. You are faced with an ethical dilemma. Do you lie to get the records or not?

People can approach ethical decision-making from different perspectives.

Those who follow a strict moral code in making decisions are called absolutists. They look to the rightness of an action, not the result of that action. They follow absolute rules regardless of the situation. In the above case, they would not lie. They would argue that the end never justifies the means. The absolutist looks for universal laws and then follows them. Absolutists look for the right action, not the right consequence. People in this category often draw on their strong religious beliefs.

Others approach the problem by looking at the consequences of their decision, not the decision itself. These people believe the end does justify the means. In the above scenario, the journalist would misrepresent himself and go undercover to get the information and expose the mayor's wrongdoing. The overriding goal of the journalist, he would argue, is to serve as watchdog of government, and lying would justify pursuing that goal.

Another ethical approach involves *situation ethics*. Those who follow this principle look at each situation and decide what to do on the basis of the facts of the case. In the above case, they might make a decision based on how likely the information would or would not implicate the mayor in a crime before making a decision about what to do.

• Ethical Models •

Ethicists have developed various methods to help us make decisions. Consider them as ways to think through a problem. Some of them include the following:

Bok's Model begins with the premise that we have empathy for others and that our goal is to achieve social trust. It analyzes an ethical problem in three steps. The first step is to consult your conscience about your situation and identify the ethical conflict. The second is to consider alternatives to solving the problem and perhaps consult an expert for advice. And the third step is to conduct a discussion with those affected, perhaps hypothetically, about the possible effects of any decision.

Kant's categorical imperative directs you to find the universal law that everyone should follow at all times and then follow it. The rule dictates how we should make our decisions. Kant believed people should act from a sense of duty. Kant, then, is an example of an absolutist. For example, one should never lie, regardless of the consequences. If everyone in the world told the truth, the assumption is the world would be a better place.

Aristotle's Golden Mean suggests we are likely to find the best decision somewhere between two extremes. For example, the journalist faced with the decision of printing a photo of a lynching victim can print a close-up or no photo at all. Or he may take the middle ground and print a long shot of the horrible event, thereby reporting the news, but not sensationalizing the situation. Unlike Kant, who focused on rules, Aristotle suggested ethics lay with the actor, and so the ethical person had to exercise practical wisdom and decide the matter on the basis of good and unchanging character traits.

Utilitarianism focuses on making the decision that results in the greatest good for the greatest number. This philosophy is probably at the core of most decisions in journalism. The focus is more on what benefits the group than the individual. For example, we publish the name of the bank president charged with embezzlement even though we know it will ruin his reputation and hurt his family, but also knowing the people in the community need to know about the safety of their money.

Pluralism starts with the idea that different values are competing for our attention in making an ethical decision. This theory requires us to consider all values and arrive at the one rule or the various rules that are most important given the situation. Use of this theory requires discernment. The values include being loyal or honest, correcting wrongs, being grateful, being just, helping others, improving one's self, and not hurting others. For example, if you promise to meet a source for lunch but your mother gets hurt and needs your help, you would conclude that helping an injured person is more important than keeping your word to have lunch.

Communitarianism helps us make ethical decisions when facing societal problems. We are all part of a community and owe a certain allegiance to that community for the benefits it provides us. Communitarians look to the effect ethical decisions have on the community. Social justice is paramount. Political and social concerns override personal interests, though they do not ignore them. Communitarianism helps remind journalists they need to focus on something larger than themselves. For example, putting in a new shopping mall might help the local economy, but if the city has to raze and displace a large neighborhood to do it, the question becomes which will harm or benefit the community the most and what do we do with the residents who no longer have homes if we raze their houses?

The Potter Box is used to help us determine where our loyalties lie in ethical decision-making. The process involves a four-part test. First, you must understand the facts of the situation, including the ethical dilemma. Second, what are your values and which values are most important? Third, apply various ethical principles discussed above to see what conclusion you reach about what to do. The more principles reach the same conclusion, the more likely your decision may be the right one. Fourth, determine your loyalties. Are there competing loyalties? After working through all steps of the model, you are in a better position to make a judgment on what to do.

• Ethical Codes •

Ethics, like law and morality, ultimately helps us with our behavior. Many professions, including journalism, have codes of ethics that dictate the expected behavior of those in the professions. (*The Society of Professional Journalists' Code of Ethics* is in the appendix of this book.) By following codes of ethics, people recognize us as members of a particular group that is known to behave in a certain way. The codes help establish reputation and identity. Ultimately, these codes are guides that also help us make decisions that support the values of those professions.

Some ethical codes have the force of law for some professions. For example, if lawyers violate their code of ethics they can lose their license to practice law. Journalists, on the other hand, are expected to be ethical, but if they're not, the government can't come in and tell them they can't be journalists. That's because the First Amendment prohibits the government from interfering in a citizen's right of expression. Government control of the media poses a greater threat to freedom than unethical journalism.

• Ethical Problems of the Press •

Journalists face a host of problems that affect credibility today other than those discussed above. Here is a list of some of them:

- *Pack journalism*, where journalists — afraid of losing out to their competition — report only what everyone else reports, making it more difficult for readers and viewers to put things in context because the reporters fail to show different perspectives of the story.
- *Race horse journalism* focuses on who's winning or losing an election instead of on the underlying reasons and issues that need to be discussed.
- Emphasizing conflict for dramatic purposes, instead of focusing on possible solutions to problems, can undermine people's views of

democracy. Focusing on the watchdog role of journalists is important, but the Press may have a greater role serving as a guide dog in a complex society.

- The paparazzi give all journalists a bad name. Practicing *keyhole journalism* and invading the privacy of others is reprehensible. And watching a bunch of crazed journalists in a feeding frenzy is more akin to mad dog journalism than watchdog journalism. Invasion of privacy decisions fall into three categories: Need to know. Right to know. Want to know. The most justifiable reason for getting information is when there is a need to know because the information affects others in some way. Right to know simply gives the reporter a legal reason for intruding, though not necessarily an ethical one. Want to know is the least ethically justifiable reason for seeking private information. It borders on voyeurism.

- *Yellow journalism* is the use of cheaply sensational methods to attract readers and should be avoided regardless of the platform.

- Conflicts of interest, real or perceived, interfere with the objectivity and believability of the journalist. Receiving gifts, developing friendships with news subjects, taking outside jobs, joining causes, and the like must be avoided. Participating in the news is a direct conflict of interest. Using news helicopters to do the job of police or withholding information from the public at the behest of authorities may seem like the civic thing to do, but it can lead to outside control of the Press and a loss of trust. The police have their job to do, and journalists have theirs. It's best to keep the pursuits separate.

- Plagiarism should be avoided.

- Misuse of quotes is unethical. Quotes should always be attributed, appear in quotation marks, and never be altered. If you must alter the words, drop the quote marks and paraphrase. Attribution is still necessary.

- Paying for news sets a bad precedent that undermines credibility and the basic principles of the democracy. Such costs are passed on to the audience in the form of higher advertising rates and subscription costs. As we raise prices, we cut out the poorest segment of society from getting news and participating in political dialogue since they can no longer afford the information necessary to join in the discussion. Prior to the Enlightenment only the wealthy could afford information, effectively disenfranchising a large part of society. Such action makes the concept of democracy impossible. Historically, subscription costs have been kept low so all can get information and participate.

- Tearing down the ethical wall separating the news and advertising departments establishes a conflict of interest. Some advertising departments now conduct reader surveys to find out what people want to read and then play an important role in deciding what news gets printed. This practice undermines the credibility of the Press by suggesting to readers that journalists can be bought, and that the only news people will get is the news that will profit the media.
- Withholding information usually indicates a conflict of interest. The only time a journalist should not report pertinent information is when he isn't sure the information is correct, in which case he should find out.
- Making a mistake and not correcting it undermines trust. Make sure everyone sees you correct errors, whether it's on air or in print. People make mistakes. Most of us are ready to forgive those who admit them and correct them. It also tells the audience that you're paying attention to your work and trying to get it right. That goes a long way to building trust.

• Mass Media Effects •

As already noted, ethical journalists in facing these and other problems need to be concerned not just with individual ethical decisions, but with the overall affect of their reporting on society as well. Mass communication researchers have long been concerned with how the news media affects the way we think and act, as well as how we determine truth.

The problem has been compounded by the amount of messages we receive. By some estimates we now get more messages from all media — news, advertising, etc. — in a year than our grandparents did in a lifetime. On average, Americans consume four hours of conventional media a day, and if you add new media, it's closer to eight hours a day.

Critics suggest that the media exploits and reinforces stereotypes, demonstrates anti-social behavior, and promotes violence. Others, however, defend the media as giving us a way to release negative energy, learn more about our world, and promote socialization.

In the early twentieth century, Walter Lippmann, a renowned social scientist and journalist, suggested the news media played a significant role in influencing our perception of reality. Lippmann said in his book, *Public Opinion*, that journalists' stories are constructs of an event that produce *images in our head*. He said the media arouse feelings — good and bad — about an event through these mental images. These feelings are powerful forces in how people perceive truth. And the stronger our emotions are tied to the mental image, the more we believe or don't believe the image is true.

In a sense, Lippmann said we create our own reality in our minds about an event based on the images provided by the media. We compare them with our own set of rules, values, and judgments developed from past experience. If what the media tells us conflicts with our beliefs, we are bothered and have to find more information from trusted sources to help us understand the new information in light of what we already know, value, and believe. We thereby tend to reinforce our preconceived ideas and construct our own view of what is true. What we believed in the past then affects what we believe in the future.

The danger is that by relying on past perceptions and the strong emotional attachments they create, we are less likely to think critically about our perceptions and how we use them to interpret the new information. This is not only a problem for the receiver of the information but the reporter as well, since he is also filtering his reporting through his past knowledge, values, and beliefs.

Add to this problem the pressure of news deadlines, the focus on profit, and the need to deliver the news ever faster and the journalist often gives little thought to how his story affects his audience or how he is personally influencing the story. And the public is in the same situation, failing to check their accepted beliefs in light of new information and seeking only those news sources that mirror their preconceptions of what is true.

With the general public now contributing to today's news coverage via Twitter, Facebook, blogs, and other forms of social media, control of the flow of news and information is shifting from trained journalists to the public at large. As a result, the credibility problem is compounded since the news now is tainted even more with opinion, personal bias, and distortion, making critical analysis and self-introspection on both the part of the "journalist" and the audience more elusive and the acquisition of truth less likely.

• Exercise •

Review the *SPJ Code of Ethics* in the appendix and identify examples in the news where the media has violated each area of the code. How would you correct each problem?

News reporters often have a difficult time defining just what news is. One definition may be that it's **a chronicle of current events, issues, and people that is of interest to a general audience**. But it probably deserves a closer look to really understand what that means.

• Elements of News •

If the Press exists to help us find truth, and truth comes from knowing, and knowing comes from being curious, what are those things that make us curious? Although different people may be curious about different things, we have discovered some universal characteristics about what it is that makes us want to know. In journalism we call these the *elements of news*, and they help us define just what news is. All stories have some or all of them, or they are not stories.

Audience — The characteristic all journalists must first consider when gathering news is audience. That is, who is going to receive the information? News will be relevant or interesting, or neither, depending upon who gets it.

If a new sewer project is under way in Columbus, Ohio, the residents there are more likely to find the information useful and interesting because it will affect their lives. It may disrupt traffic, delay their water service, increase their taxes, or, they hope, improve their sewer service. The people of Columbus, Georgia, meanwhile, could care less. It neither affects them nor interests them. Obviously, therefore, the journalist in Georgia would not print a news story about the sewer project in Ohio. It's simply the wrong audience for the story.

Impact — We are all interested in things that might help or hurt us, as just noted. We call this impact. If the school is going to raise your tuition, you want to know about it because it's going to affect your pocketbook. If the city is going to tear up your street for a sewer project, it will affect you. If the project is in a different city, chances are it won't affect you, and you won't care. Every story has impact on someone. The questions are who is affected, how much, and why. Journalists must understand the impact in each story before they begin to write it.

Conflict — Probably the first thing English teachers talk about when it comes to storytelling is conflict. In fact, it is a necessary ingredient in all stories. That's because we read stories to find out what happens. If there is no conflict, there's no need to keep reading, nothing is to be determined. Conflict comes in many forms. It may include man against man, man against nature, man against himself, nation against nation, etc.

Novelty — It is often said that when a dog bites a man it is not news, but when a man bites a dog, that is certainly news. Why? One is an ordinary event in most instances. The second is quite rare, unusual, bizarre, and, consequently, interesting. In fact, most news is about something that is out of the ordinary. Contrary to popular opinion, most of the world is not falling apart. Most people go about their daily lives without the turmoil we see on the evening news. They work, raise a family, and live an ordinary life. They may get their name in the paper when they are born, when they get married, and when they die. The fact that we see turmoil in the news is precisely because it is unusual in most instances. It is ironic, then, that bad news in the newspaper and on air should provide us with some consolation. It should remind us that bad news is still out of the ordinary.

Prominence — Let's face it, the more important you are, the more newsworthy you are. We admire people who have accomplished greater things than we have been able to accomplish, and we want to know who they are and, perhaps, how they did it. We are also curious about those who have become notorious, which is a form of prominence in terms of their news value because we want to know how they messed up. As we just noted, prominence is itself unusual. Of course, there are degrees of prominence. The local Boy Scout who receives an award has achieved a degree of prominence, at least for a moment. In short, journalists should remember that news is about people.

Proximity — As we noted with audience, the closer you are to an event — the more proximate — the greater your interest, and the greater the news value of that event. Most people are more concerned with what happens close to home than on the other side of the world. And if something does happen a long way away, they are more interested in it if the journalist can tell them how it affects them. Consequently, journalists are often told to localize an event to bring it home and make it more relevant to their news audience. If an earthquake rocks China, for example, the journalist may focus on how a local tour group traveling in China has fared. If Iran cuts foreign oil exports, what does that mean for gas prices at the local pump?

Timeliness — If I run into a room and yell, "Guess what? Nixon resigned," you're going to wonder what I'm smoking. News is, by definition, new. And even if it involves old information, there must be some new aspect about it, or it's simply not news. To be relevant, people must have timely information to be able to participate in their world. It is important to know about an upcoming play at the local theatre or what the legislature is doing before you can attend the performance or make your wishes known to your representative. Tomorrow is too late. This poses a problem for the journalist who may be tempted in the digital age to publish first and worry about accuracy later. It's still better to be slow and right than fast and wrong. Ultimately, news is not news if it's wrong. And to be wrong means to be discredited and, ultimately, unread.

Although each news story must contain at least one of these elements to be newsworthy, it is also true that stories often contain more than one news element. Sometimes a story may contain all of them. When that happens, the story's news value increases because there are more things about which to be curious. It is important to remember, however, that the facts dictate just how many news elements exist in each story and how much impact, etc., each has, and to resist the temptation to embellish and sensationalize.

• Need to Know vs. Want to Know •

In looking at these characteristics we notice that they are all intertwined — that is, audience is determined by impact, proximity often affects prominence, and so on — and that they fall into two general categories — news that we *need to know* and news that we *want to know*. In a democratic society, conscientious journalists provide the reader, viewer, and listener with both types of information to fulfill their Constitutional mandate to foster an Enlightenment-based society that uses information to help citizens find the truth about their world. It isn't enough that journalists just give their audience what they want to know because in the long run what happens between countries is more important than what happens with the current pop star. Consequently, those in the Press who understand this work to make sure they know and appreciate the relative importance of each story they run.

It must be noted that not all in the Press fall into this category, of course. Some pander, instead, to the sensational and trivial in an effort to secure ratings and circulation figures in the pursuit of profit alone, as noted in the last chapter. As a result, important news often gets lost. When that happens, the news menus become predictable and trite. Viewers turn on the news and see the same kinds of stories about brush fires, car wrecks, and crime and little or no information about government and other "boring" stories discarded for lack of exciting video. In the end, such a diet leaves readers empty, misguided about their community and country, and cynical about the news and those who report it, and ratings and circulation numbers eventually fall or stagnate for lack of relevance and variety. One can watch the news or go bowling, they figure. It's just another entertainment venue. If it weren't for the important role of the Press in the democracy, that perception likely wouldn't matter, but the Founders gave it a more central role, even going so far as to protect it in the Bill of Rights. Journalists who care about their communities give their audience news that's not only exciting, but important, "boring" or not.

• Types of Stories •

Although all stories contain some, if not all, of the elements of news just discussed, stories are nevertheless often told in different ways. Just as those in an English class learn about the novel, or the short story, or the play; those in journalism also employ different formats depending upon the kind of story they are telling. This book will explain some of them in detail later. Largely, the facts and purpose of the story dictate which method the journalist uses.

News story – The news story is the principal format used by the news media to deliver the news. Most of the stories you see in a newspaper and on the air fall into this category. These stories are usually short and to the point, and designed to answer who, what, when, where, why, and how of every news event, with most of those questions answered near the beginning of the story. Whether the news is delivered by print or broadcast, the receiver should understand the story quickly. Brevity is important because time and space in the media is generally limited (except for the web) and because people are busy and want the news quickly. Yet despite its brevity, the information should still be complete and in context. Commentary, off-hand remarks, raised eyebrows, idle talk, gestures, and anything that would indicate the reporter's personal thoughts about the story are unethical and to be avoided. The purpose is to provide people with objective, complete, and unbiased information and allow them to reach their own conclusions about the story. News stories look and sound like this:

> *An Oklahoma City man was killed in a two-car accident Tuesday at Hefner and Rockwell Roads after police said he ran a red light.*

Notice that who, what, when, where, why, and how have all been generally addressed. The details will follow later in the story. The purpose of a news story is to simply, directly tell you the news.

Feature story — The feature story looks and sounds more like a short story. It has a beginning, middle, and formal ending that usually ties back somehow into the beginning. The purpose of a feature story is to focus on someone or something of interest and to show rather than tell. Feature writers use words to make you use your senses. They want you to see, taste, smell, feel, and hear the story. Feature stories are usually timeless, that is, they could be of interest now or next week or next month. They may look at the shoeshine man at the airport, some aspect of local history, or a homicide detective known for his ability to solve cases. Feature stories look and sound like this:

> *The dark brown loafers, creased and cracked at the toe and rubbed raw at the heels, looked like they'd seen 100 miles of bad road. "Man, I ain't seen anyone more in need of a shine."*

It is important to report just facts, as in news stories, but in feature stories the reporter selects facts that make the reader see the story and the people in them.

News-feature story — The news-feature story, as the name notes, is a combination of news and feature. It is written much the same way a feature is written, but it has a news element to it. Therefore, unlike the feature, it is timely. News-feature stories are often used to help us see, hear, feel, etc., an event. They are often used in conjunction with a news story to show some aspect of the larger story or to characterize the participants in a story. Let's say an old woman was robbed and beaten in her home. We could do a straight news story and tell you what happened, but because of the victim's age and vulnerability it might not fully capture the horror of the event. Instead, we might be able to give the reader a better picture if we use a news-feature story. Note the difference between the two and how the news-feature helps us better see what happened. First the news story:

> *An 87-year-old Oklahoma City woman was beaten and robbed of $800 Tuesday night in her home after two men broke the lock on her front door. "I never thought it would happen to me," said Ms. Billie Johnson, who lost her entire monthly social security check.*

Now the news-feature:

> *Eighty-seven-year-old Billie Johnson, rubbing her bruised and bloodied hands, sat on her front porch swing Wednesday morning and watched as the man from Ace Security put a shiny brass lock on her scarred front door.*
>
> *"I never thought it would happen to me," she said, her face drawn and tired.*

Ms. Johnson spent a night of terror in her home Tuesday after two men broke inside and beat and robbed her of $800, her entire monthly social security check.

In the first story, we're telling; in the second, we're showing.

Sidebar — A sidebar is simply some article that is related to another, more important story. The sidebar could be any kind of story. It could be another news story, a news-feature story, and editorial, anything. For that matter the main story, called the main bar, could be any kind of story, though more often than not, it's a news story. Sidebars are useful in that they can take a multi-faceted story and break it up into smaller, more manageable stories dealing with different aspects of the same story. For example, let's say an airliner crashes at the airport. The main story, of course, would be the crash. That would be the main bar. But we might do multiple sidebars on that topic. We could do a lesser-related news-feature story on how the Federal Aviation Administration and the National Transportation Safety Board investigate such crashes. We might do a news sidebar on a survivor. We might do an editorial on the need for the elimination of bird nesting sites near the airport. We might do an investigative story on the airline's safety record. All of these stories would run the same day or days after the crash, often on the same page or in a separate section covering the event. Together, they give us a bigger picture of the event. Note the following story beginnings to a main bar story and its related sidebar:

Main bar

An airliner carrying 250 passengers and crew crashed on takeoff Thursday from the municipal airport after witnesses said they saw one of the plane's engines explode as it flew into a flock of birds.

Sidebar

A baggage handler was credited with saving the lives of four passengers from the ill-fated airliner that crashed Thursday at the municipal airport after he ran into the burning wreckage and pulled them to safety.

Remember, the main bar is the main story, the reason all the other stories exist. The sidebar is just a side event or angle.

Depth story — Again, as the name implies, this story examines something in great depth or detail. These stories are useful to help us understand complex things and are becoming more the staple of newspapers because they have the staff and space to explain big, complicated topics. Since it takes longer to get breaking news in the newspaper, most people get their news as it happens from radio or TV or online. But if they want to know the details, they wait for the newspaper. Reporters have more time and space to explore and explain. Consequently, these stories are usually long and exhaustive. They may take up an entire page or section, or they may run in a series over several days or weeks. Stories that deal with science and technology are often topics of depth stories. They may explore how a volcano works or examine new discoveries about the human genome. They may explain the process — start to finish — of how to build a super highway. While there is no single method reporters use to begin writing one, they often sound like feature stories with lots of detail. For example:

> *Two hundred feet below the Antarctic ice lies a prehistoric lake filled, scientists speculate, with creatures long thought extinct.*

The story would then, in detail, explain how the lake was discovered, what might be in it, and how the scientists are going to explore it.

Investigative story — Like the depth story, the investigative story is exhaustive. In a sense, the depth and investigative stories are cousins. They are more difficult to do, and only the best and most experienced reporters are usually assigned to do them. The investigative story, more than any other, gives news organizations status and credibility and power because it makes those in power tremble. The purpose of the investigative story is to ferret out wrongdoing in business and government and wherever unbridled power can do damage, to expose it and use the power of embarrassment and citizen and consumer anger to demand correction and change. The investigative story is not a story about how the district attorney or the police are investigating something; it is when the news organization itself, using its own resources of time, money, and people, delve into the world of corruption. Reporters are often met with threats to their lives. The news organizations may be faced with lawsuits charging libel. Yet without these kinds of crusading efforts, stories like Watergate would never have come to light, and corruption and inefficient government would prevail. News organizations will often announce in the beginning paragraph that the story is investigative. For example:

The governor and two of his aides received more than $4 million in payments from two builders before construction began on the new interstate highway, a Daily Bugle *investigation of state financial records has shown.*

The following stories, although also fact-based, are subjective in that they contain views of the writer.

Editorials — An editorial is the voice of the newspaper; it is the newspaper's view on a particular subject. It can be critical or supportive of something, informative, or suggest a course of action on a particular issue. The editor or publisher often writes editorials, but at the larger papers an editorial board — a group of veteran journalists who have the experience and wisdom to warrant giving advice to the community, usually writes them. They are people who are well read and have a broad knowledge of government and history. Editorials are structured like arguments or essays. They usually start with a premise and then offer facts and opinions in support. Research indicates that editorials don't always change minds, but they do make people think. Some of the most important writing ever published in American newspapers has been in the form of editorials. *The Federalist Papers*, a series of editorials written in the early days of the Republic, persuaded the new states to ratify the Constitution. Editorials look and sound like this:

If Americans want to stop Congressional gridlock, they must elect more centrist politicians from both parties who can compromise on important issues.

Editorials, like other opinion pieces, are usually segregated in special sections of the newspaper and labeled as such so readers understand they are reading opinion and not straight factual reporting. Although editorials can appear anywhere, so long as they are labeled editorials, they most often appear on the editorial page.

Columns — A column represents a particular writer's view on something. Unlike the editorial, which is the newspaper's position on a particular subject, the column is personal. Columns are usually in a box, often with the writer's name and picture. They often have a title and may be on a particular subject, like politics, technology, or even horoscopes. The column may take on any form. It could be written in third person, first person, or second person.

Columnists often have a particularly memorable style of writing. They may have special expertise in an area, either by training, education, or experience. Like the editorial, they can appear anywhere in the paper, but they usually are found on the op-ed page — the opinion page opposite the editorial page. They sound like this:

> *When I was a kid, if you got into trouble at school, you got into trouble at home. Now everyone goes into counseling. Give me a break.*

Columnists are the celebrities of the newspaper. Today, many stories online are blogs, which are usually nothing more than online columns. These usually are not straight news stories because they contain the writers' interpretation of the news, especially if they are subjects in which the bloggers/columnists claim an interest or expertise.

Reviews — If you want to know if the new play in town is worth attending or the new book is worth reading, you may read a review. Reviews are articles that analyze and critique the merits and demerits of a play, movie, book, or other artistic creation to help the reader learn about it and decide if he wants to go see it, hear it, or read it. People who know what they're talking about write better reviews. They may be authors or playwrights or artists or musicians themselves. The best reviews are written as critiques, a form of writing that analyzes the creative experience by taking apart it's component parts and seeing how they work or don't work. For example, a play might be analyzed by looking at the play's structure, the set design, the costuming, and acting. It is more than just someone gushing over how they liked it or blowing steam over how they didn't have a good time. A well-written review might sound like this:

> *Arthur Miller likely would be proud of Circle Theatre's latest rendition of* Death of a Salesman *which brings together somber lighting, emotionally charged acting, and a stark set design that is suitable to portraying the tragedy of one man's life.*

• Choosing the News — The Budget Meeting •

Thousands of journalists write thousands of stories for print and broadcast every day. Obviously, all of these stories can't make the newspaper or the evening news. There simply isn't enough space or time. Of course, there's the Internet, which has an unlimited capacity to deliver information, so technically all of them could be published. But even if all of them were, no one would have the time to read or watch them all. People have jobs to go to and lives to live. Even a large daily newspaper contains more news than most people can digest. The number of words in a big daily newspaper is equivalent to the number of words in a novel. Let's face it — most people don't want to read a novel every day.

Time isn't the only consideration. Cost also determines how much news gets delivered. The more news that's published, the more paper and ink are needed. The more news that's broadcast on TV and radio, the more electricity is needed. Getting the news out is expensive, so journalists must be judicious in selecting only the most important and most interesting news. Consequently, they have to make choices about what goes in the paper and on the air and what doesn't.

So how do they do it? It's called the budget meeting, a time when all the editors from all the major news departments — news, sports, business, features, national and international, travel, etc. — gather daily in a big room and discuss (often argue) on how to present one day's history. The editors bring the stories that pertain to their subject areas — stories that they decided earlier needed to be covered or that their reporters have found on their own — and prioritize them based on the news values discussed earlier. Then together they try to figure out which stories they should put on the front page, on the front of each section, and on the inside.

The editors also take into consideration history and politics, the issues of the day and what is on people's minds in helping them make their decisions. They look at science and the arts and culture — everything. And they look at the Constitution and Milton and Locke and the philosophical foundation of our democracy. In other words, they attempt to organize the news based on what people need to know to govern their country and their lives. Those stories that have the greatest impact on the greatest number of people are most important and go out front so they will receive the greatest attention. Lesser stories go inside.

Not all of the news, of course, is serious. The editors attempt to give readers and viewers a balance. Too much serious information would overwhelm people. Editors understand that they also must provide information people want, not just need. And so we get news about sports and entertainment and other topics of interest. Such news entices the citizen to buy the product. He not only gets the meat and potatoes but also the dessert. As noted earlier, the problem with many news organizations is that they are heavy on dessert and light on the meat and potatoes.

• Exercise •

Test students' understanding of the different kinds of stories by cutting a selection of stories from a large daily newspaper and allowing the students to identify the various types noted above.

Then test their news judgment by taking at least a dozen of the stories, including several news stories from the front page and inside, and having them conduct their own budget meeting to determine which news should go on the front page, on the front of each section, and on the inside pages. Make them explain their decisions based on the Elements of News and their understanding of current events, history, and Enlightenment philosophy. Then compare and discuss their choices with the editors' choices in the newspaper.

• Characteristics and Skills of a Journalist •

Reporters are inherently curious and find the world interesting. They want to know what's going on so they can share this knowledge with others. They believe people will be able to live better lives if they are informed. Some reporters also may be motivated by a desire to right wrongs and improve society, thus following the old reporter's adage that "the role of a journalist is to comfort the afflicted and afflict the comfortable."

In fact, given the founding principles of The Enlightenment and the idea of democratic rule, one of the hallmarks of a libertarian society is the ability for people to challenge authority and the status quo, to change when society or circumstances dictate a need for change.

Nevertheless, journalists are trained to let the facts and not personal bias guide them when righting perceived wrongs. Ultimately, it is the not the journalist's job to prosecute. It is the job of the journalist to inform others so they can be empowered to change things for themselves. Journalists do this by comparing society's customs and laws to how things really work and then informing the public of any differences between the two. Put another way, when you're driving down the road and have a flat, you don't get out of the car and admire the three tires that are still up. You get busy fixing the flat. Society expects the car to roll smoothly down the road according to its laws and customs. If that doesn't happen, society needs to know about it. The job of a journalist, therefore, is to let people know about the flat, so they can choose to fix it and continue on their way.

Of course, the journalist must be prepared for society to ignore the flat and do nothing. Years ago, journalists informed people in a certain state that their congressman had hired a secretary who had no secretarial skills but who had other attributes he liked. Once her shortcomings were revealed, he left office in disgrace only to be elected again by the same citizens he had duped. Ultimately, the power of change belongs to the people — whether they choose to exercise it or not.

Journalists are also teachers, and so they must possess the ability to explain things well to others without talking down to them or over their heads. The challenge is to be able to explain complex issues to the mechanic with an eighth grade education as well as to the physician with years of schooling, and to do it in such a way that both understand the topic completely. This requires an ability to understand the big picture of any idea or event, to be able to cut to the heart of any issue, and it means the reporter must be able to synthesize facts and present them clearly, completely, concisely, and in context. These are not easy tasks. Have you ever met someone who couldn't give directions, who couldn't tell a joke, who couldn't explain something? These people would not make good reporters.

In addition to being inquisitive and able to explain things to others, journalists need to be well educated in government, history, law, science, math, language, philosophy, art, music, drama, sociology, psychology — in others words, in everything. The reason is simple: you don't know what you're going to have to explain to someone tomorrow, and if you don't understand it yourself, you can't explain it to others. Journalists are the last Renaissance people — they often have a strong liberal arts education. Remember, the journalist's job is to explain the world to a busy citizenry that often doesn't have the time, ability, or inclination to go find out on their own. This doesn't mean taking on a paternalistic role and dictating to others what they should think. It means providing them with the information so they can make informed decisions for themselves.

Obviously, to be fully educated, it is also important that news people keep up with current events. After all, that's news. How can you tell others what's going on if you don't know yourself? Journalists typically are news junkies. They are constantly reading, watching, and listening to the news on air, online, and in print. After a while, they become so in tune with the nature of news, that many can often predict where big stories will occur next simply by watching where events are brewing.

For most journalists, a day begins by getting online and checking email and news sites. Over breakfast, they watch the morning news shows. On the way to work, they listen to the radio — for news. Once at work, they scan the major daily newspapers from around the country and overseas. They look for the news and how it's reported. Different cultures look at news differently and emphasize different aspects of a story. To put news in context, it's important to take these different perspectives into consideration.

Journalists typically are skeptical people. They follow the old Chicago newspaper adage: "You say your mother loves you? Check it out!" Journalists take no one's word for anything — not even Mom's. Journalists demand facts, confirmation, and proof. They even tell readers and viewers where they got the information. So if readers want to check the information themselves, they can. For this reason, listing sources in the story is very important. It increases the journalist's credibility. It's the journalist saying, "Look I'm so confident of this that I'll tell you where I got it. If you don't believe me, go check it out yourself."

Journalists aren't trying to be difficult by demanding confirmation, but they understand that if they get something wrong it can affect a lot of people adversely, as well as their own credibility. Again, like the little boy who yelled wolf when no wolf existed, after a while, no one will believe you if you get it wrong. Journalists have two things to sell — their ability and training in gathering and delivering the news, and their credibility. Lose either and you're finished.

Being skeptical doesn't mean being cynical, a problem many veteran journalists face after years of being skeptical. Journalists must be on guard against this because cynicism is inherently biased. A cynic is someone who has made up his mind about something before listening to the facts; he's already decided something is bad. A skeptic is someone with an open mind who says "I'm ready to listen, but prove what you say." Often, journalists become cynical after spending years listening to people lie to them. As a result, if they are not careful, they grow to assume all people lie all the time.

Unfortunately, this attitude occurs because people often try to use the Press to their own advantage. Sometimes they don't want people to know what they are doing because it may be against the law or because they may want to manipulate people, whether for selfish or unselfish reasons; so they lie and attempt to mislead the Press. Politicians and others in power often fall into this category. Journalists must be constantly on guard against this. For this reason, journalists are always skeptical of powerful people. They understand that uncontrolled power from any sector is dangerous.

As a result, in addition to everything else, a journalist first and foremost must be intelligent. Journalists can't be naïve; they must be clever and street smart. They should not, as some politicians wish, be stenographers with amnesia, parroting what people say without challenge or explanation. A journalist is not a tape recorder. Neither is he there to offer his own opinion in news stories or reach conclusions for others. Though his job is not to argue with sources, his job is always to make people explain themselves and point out any inconsistencies in what they say. This requires preparation and thought before every interview.

Obviously then, those in the Press must be open and honest themselves if their goal is to help people get at the truth. For the Press to be useful, it must be believed. Any activities that detract from that goal should be avoided. More, they must not only be honest, they also must look honest. Even the appearance of impropriety should be avoided. Sources, as well as readers, viewers, and listeners, should understand where the journalist is coming from, what information he is looking for, and the reason for asking for it. There should be no hidden agendas, no agendas whatsoever except for finding out what's going on. Questions should be designed to help the journalist understand the story as it emerges from the facts, not as a means of reaching his own preconceived conclusion about something.

Toward this end, journalists must be fair. To understand any idea or event, it is important to get all sides of the story and keep opinion out of the reporting. It is important that journalists understand their own biases and to keep an eye on them so those biases don't creep into their stories. An editor should be able to send a trained journalist who personally believes in a woman's right to choose to have an abortion to an anti-abortion rally and have the reporter cover it in such a way that no one can tell what her personal opinion is on the issue.

Journalists must practice accuracy. Getting close isn't good enough. Even one small error in a story is fatal. It makes the reader question the entire piece. It makes him ask: "If the journalist got this wrong, what else did he get wrong?" Consequently, journalists need to check all their information, including the spelling of names, the results of their math, and the accuracy of their sources. Journalists must understand their story before they write it, and then review it to see if they have accurately said what they thought they said.

It follows that journalists must understand language. They must be able to write well and understand both the denotation and connotation of words and the shades of meaning they can convey. A journalist's primary instruction is in learning where to find information and how to convey it accurately. Think of the difference it makes to say "Jesus walked on water" rather than "Jesus walked in water." All we did was change one letter, and the result is a world religion. Unfortunately, many people throw around words as if they don't matter. The journalist must consider the precise meaning of each word he uses.

Even the way a sentence is written, the order in which words are placed, matters, because varying the words and structure changes what is emphasized and that shades meaning. Think of the difference between Fox News and MSNBC. They may cover the same stories, but the way in which they write and deliver the story often conveys different perspectives, emotional and factual, of the same event.

Journalists should be empathetic. Not sympathetic. Sympathy means you feel sorry for someone. When you do that you take sides; you become biased. To say on the air "We have a sad story for you tonight." is technically unethical because the journalist is no longer reporting objectively. In fact, he's not reporting at all, he's interpreting. He's not telling you the facts and letting you decide the meaning and importance and truth of the story. He is short-circuiting the process by offering his own opinion and analysis of it without calling it that. The journalist should just give us the facts. We'll decide for ourselves if the story is sad or not.

The Journalist's Primer

Empathy, on the other hand, means the journalist is able to put himself in other people's shoes, to see and understand something from another person's perspective. To be able to fully report a story, one must be able to see and understand different sides of the story without taking sides in the story.

Years ago, I had an editor who sent me out into the middle of nowhere in central Florida to cover a dispute between homeowners. I drove through miles of scrub pine to get to a cul-de-sac surrounded by houses. I parked the car, got out and went to the first house and knocked on the door. I explained to the resident who I was and asked if he could tell me about the dispute. He said he could, but that to understand it I would need to come out and sit on the curb and survey the situation from his vantage point. I said OK and went out to sit on the curb with him. Once he was finished explaining the situation I thanked him and decided in my own mind that he certainly had summed up the story logically. But to be fair and get a complete understanding of the story, I knew that I had to talk to the other residents as well. Oddly, as I made my way around to the different houses and talked to the different owners, each of them required me to come out and sit on the curb and see the situation from a different and personal perspective. Each time I physically moved, I put myself in their shoes and saw the situation from their unique point of view, and each time I did, the story changed, and, from their perspective, each viewpoint made sense. Frustrated, I got back into the car and drove back to the newspaper. I wasn't sure what I was going to tell the editor, so I just went back to my desk and worked on something else. Finally, the editor ordered me into his office and asked me what I had learned. I cleared my throat and told him that as far as I could tell they were all telling the truth as they saw it, that the story and truth changed as I put myself in each person's shoes and saw the situation from their perspective. The editor told me that if I remembered that lesson I would make a good journalist. It was a lesson I never forgot.

This doesn't mean that there are no right and wrong answers and that every point of view is correct. People who claim they have a right to their own opinion may be right as far as it goes; the idea, however, that their opinion is as valid as the next guy's is not necessarily true. It does mean that the more perspectives you have and the more facts you gather, the easier it will be for the reader, viewer, or listener to find the truth among those competing facts and perspectives. He said-she said stories are useless. Get more facts until the reader can find out what the truth is.

Finally, journalists must understand that the reader, viewer, and listener are their ultimate concern. That means always putting their understanding first. To say that Congress is going to raise taxes by $1 billion is meaningless. Few can understand that amount. Rather, the journalist should say that a $1 billion hike will mean approximately a $3.33 increase for every man, woman and child in the country. That figure we can understand.

Journalists who care for their audience dig deep for the facts. Too often, journalists practice surface reporting — using only the information that can be gathered easily, thus denying the citizen important information that can put the story in context. Journalists who fail to look behind the scenes often miss the real story. Public relation releases that offer only one side should be used only as a starting place to get the full story, not as the finished product. One source is good, two are better, and more are best.

• Educational Needs for the New Century •

If journalists are the eyes and ears of our world, they need to be intelligent, educated people. But this doesn't mean just any kind of education will do.

Unfortunately, in our culture education is designed primarily to help people get a job. It is more about training than education. The reason for this is fairly obvious. First, we are a highly complex, specialized, capitalistic society. To keep the economy going, we need a strong, intelligent workforce — one that obviously needs to be well trained. Second, students who spend thousands of dollars on school need and expect a return on that investment, especially if they've borrowed the money to go to school in the first place.

But there's more at stake than just money. The economy won't matter much if we fail to maintain the democracy and the institutions that provide for it. First, we need to distinguish between training and education. Training is about learning to do a task. Trained people must constantly be retrained as the task or the technology changes. Educated people are able to figure out things as they go. They are knowledgeable about the world and they have become skilled in logic and analytical thought. They have become problem solvers, thinkers, and creators. They are more than trained. An educated person, whether he has a well-paying job or not, has more than just money. In a sense, he owns the future because he knows the past. Education is its own reward. Educated people are leaders because they understand the world — all of it, and they can put it into context. They understand how the parts relate to the whole, and so they are better able to figure things out.

I knew a brilliant physician once who understood everything about his area of medicine, but get him on another subject and he was clueless. Just because you're smart and well trained doesn't mean you are well educated.

Many of our colleges today are designed as training centers. As I told one of my colleagues: "We're no longer professors; we're economic facilitators." Students major in business or science or some other area, but know little, if anything, about the liberal arts — the foundation of democracy. Many of them aren't interested in learning about it.

For people living in a free, democratic society who mean to be their own governors, it is essential that they be educated so they can be good citizens as well as good workers. For those who would mean to provide them with the information and knowledge of the world around them — the journalists — it is critical.

Having noted the difference between education and training, it's still important that people be trained in whatever career they pursue. No one would want an educated carpenter working on his house who wasn't skilled in his craft. So too, it wouldn't be advisable for a highly advanced, technical democracy to rely on getting its information from an untrained journalist — citizen journalism notwithstanding. Trained journalists, as we have noted, are skilled in language and how to find and verify information and report that information in context.

We are in the midst of an information age. Knowledge is increasing exponentially. As we begin a new millennium, it will take a highly educated and trained populace to maintain a free society. It will take people who understand the past and what it means, who have the capacity to problem solve and not just follow narrow understandings. Journalists must be leaders in this endeavor by virtue of their training and education.

• Preparing to Work in New Media •

As the number of traditional journalism jobs diminish, more beginning journalists will be attracted to citizen journalism and other forms of delivery formats. No doubt as technology advances, even more opportunities will open.

To prepare for this uncertain future, and the growing fragmentation of media, those in all areas of mass communication will need to become skilled in those traditional print and broadcast areas, as well as new technology. This concept, again fueled by economics and the desire to do more with less people, is the staple of a growing number of college mass communication programs and accounts for the movement toward media convergence, requiring journalists to be able to write for print, online, and broadcast, also edit, photograph, add audio, and shoot video regardless of whether they work in print, broadcasting, online, or in any other delivery system. In essence, they must learn to do it all and all at the same time, placing news online, on air, and in the newspaper.

The danger is that many journalists, news outlets, and journalism educational programs will focus on technology and forget the basics of effective communication. In the end, it's still most important that journalists understand the basics of quality, comprehensive, objective information gathering and reporting. If you can't do that, it won't matter how much technology you know.

• The Rise of Citizen Journalism •

The future of the news business is headed in the direction of a new brand of reporting called *citizen journalism* where anyone, whether trained in information gathering or not, is encouraged to gather and publish. In a sense, it represents the democratization of information.

To be accurate, it's not really a new form of journalism. Pamphleteers — early citizen journalists who had access to a printing press — provided news and information during the nation's formative years. But it's spreading rapidly again because of changes in technology. Made possible by the advent of the Internet, this type of reporting allows anyone with a computer or camera phone to upload information anytime, anywhere and distribute it worldwide instantaneously.

In the hands of a trained journalist, the Internet is simply another way to deliver information using all of the tools the journalist relies on in the first place to make sure the story is accurate. In and of itself, this new technology does not preclude anyone from checking facts, sources, and pausing to consider the ramifications of what they are reporting. One of the benefits of newspapers is that there is a time lag between the moment when information is gathered and when it is written, edited, and again when it is published. But the temptation in the electronic age, especially in the hands of someone who has not had this training, is to publish first and ask questions later, an action that can do untold damage.

This is not to say a society of reporters would not be useful. Citizens with phones can click off a few photos without anyone knowing in a place where a journalist would attract attention and perhaps be prohibited from getting the information. Citizens can fill in when journalists aren't around. If a plane crashes, chances are someone with a camera phone is there to uplink the photos and text to their own site or to a news organization willing to use them. It's literally news as it happens. In a democracy, more accurate information is better.

Unfortunately, the story might not be accurate; it might be out of context or completely wrong. For example, the man on the street clicks off a few pictures of a riot in some Middle Eastern city, but fails to note that the incident is isolated, or worse, staged for the cameras, because he hasn't studied the political situation or the culture to know the deeper story. The result is a distortion of what's really going on. Worse, someone more malicious could post a false report about a bank failure, setting off a run on the financial markets.

Citizen journalism is taking different forms. The audience participation model encourages readers and viewers to post comments at the end of reporters' stories or to write their own stories and post photos directly to the news organization's website. More news organizations are using this method to gather information and improve the marketing of their product. But as a result, traditional journalists are finding that their roles are changing. In addition to finding and writing their own stories, they now must edit those stories and photos coming in from Cindy Citizen.

A growing number of citizen journalists are starting personal news websites called *blogs*. *The Drudge Report* is one example. Blogs often tend to offer a mixture of fact and opinion and resemble columns. Bloggers comment on what they report and give their own perspective of the story. Other citizen journalist efforts resemble community bulletin boards where anyone with the electronic means can post information.

Since most citizen journalists do not have the budget to do large investigative pieces or travel overseas, they usually focus on the local community or niche journalism that deals with a particular subject matter or area of expertise. Many are nonprofit, though some of those who have their own blogs have attracted enough advertisers to produce a respectable income.

Citizen journalism probably won't replace traditional *legacy* media. The citizen journalist can't cover the news with the same breadth and depth that traditional media can. The concern, however, is that citizen journalists, untrained in objective reporting, will muddy the line between fact and opinion and leave their audience even more challenged to find the truth.

Given the technology and the economic constraints on the news business, citizen journalism is here to stay. The wise thing to do would be to figure out how to use it well. Perhaps in the future school curricula will include a required course in information gathering and sharing for all citizens to help them understand the difference between fact and opinion, reporting and commentary.

• Exercise •

Have students identify their biases and those things about which they feel strongly. Then have them listen to someone give a speech or report on a topic with which they personally disagree. Have them try to objectively report on what was said and have the class critique their report for bias. Afterwards, ask the class how the bias could have been avoided.

CHAPTER

5

Newsgathering

Reporting is a two-step process. First we gather the information, then we organize it, write it, and report it. This requires two separate skills: the ability to know where to look for news and how to get it — primarily from documents and people — and the ability to write well. Effective journalists must be able to do both.

Obviously, we start by gathering the news first. News organizations have come up with different ways of doing this by focusing on different methods of newsgathering.

• Beats •

Most traditional journalists fall into one of two categories. They are either beat reporters or general assignment reporters. A beat reporter is assigned a specific place or subject matter to cover called a *beat*, whereas, a general assignment reporter covers whatever he is assigned or can find on his own.

The Journalist's Primer

Beats include the police and fire departments and other emergency organizations, city hall, the state legislature, the courts, the White House, Congress, the Department of Defense, and all manner of other local, state, and federal offices and agencies, in addition to various subject areas, such as health, education, sports, and anyplace else or anything else that generates news of concern to the community on a regular basis. The idea is that some places and subjects are so important that they need to be checked on a daily basis because events there have a profound effect on so many people. Most beats are standard to all news organizations because they have had a long history of generating news.

The reporters who are assigned to beats are often experts in the area they cover or they become experts over time as they cover them. For example, at large, prominent news organizations the reporter who covers courts may himself be an attorney while the reporter who covers medicine may be a physician. If you cover the financial markets on Wall Street, you need more than a degree in journalism. Chances are you have an MBA or master's degree in finance. Even those reporters who have no such training gain deep insight and expertise with experience. Many go on to write books about their subject area or are consulted for their knowledge by others who wish to gain insight into their area.

Ironically, beginning reporters often start their careers by covering one of the more important beats — obituaries. The obits page is one of the more widely read pages in the newspaper. And reporters who misspell names hear about it — loudly — from readers. Reporters start here because it teaches them a variety of important basic skills. They must be fast, accurate, and sensitive to people who are going through very difficult times. It takes a great deal of tact to be able to talk to people and get them to provide details of a loved one who has just died. People under stress react in different ways. They may express their sorrow by being sad, angry, talkative, or quiet. The beginning reporter must learn to adapt quickly and effectively to every attitude, not get defensive, and always be polite. News is ultimately about people, and understanding basic psychology is essential.

Before one begins to cover a beat, most journalists will try to bring themselves up to speed on the area by reading about it and talking to experts in the field or to other reporters who covered it before they did. For most journalists the learning curve is rather short. By virtue of their education, they are expected to pick up on things quickly.

The typical beat reporter will spend most of his day talking to people at his beat, looking for news and getting to know the procedures and politics of the office. Over time he will learn which people to trust, as well as those people not to trust. He will learn who has the power and who doesn't, who is on the inside and who is on the out, who knows what's going on, who makes a good source, and who may be trying to use him for their own purposes or block him from getting information. Journalism is a people game. If you don't like or understand people, chances are you're in the wrong field.

Beat reporting has its problems. Journalists who cover a beat for a long time may get too close to their sources, jeopardizing their ability to report accurately and objectively. The trick is to make sure everyone understands why you are there, that you will treat everyone fairly and honestly, but that you will report the news — whether it's perceived as good or bad — fairly and completely. Journalists who can maintain this attitude and communicate it to their sources gain credibility and respect. Those who become too chummy with sources find themselves in an awkward position when they have to report on something that's embarrassing.

Beat reporting also can make the journalist forget the larger world around him by becoming too focused on just one area of news. This can make it more difficult for him to report in context or cause him to fall into using the lingo or technical language associated with his beat, confusing others. Reporters must remember that just because they are familiar with a subject, their readers, viewers, and listeners may not be, and the journalist can often end up talking over their heads.

Journalists learn quickly that each beat has its own culture and it brings with it specific rules, expectations, and protocol. Often these are unwritten. It's rather like being a member of a club. A journalist is expected to behave as a journalist and maintain a professional detachment from those he covers. Nevertheless, he is expected to understand the rules and protocol of the organization.

The specific nature of each beat will pose unique newsgathering problems. Journalists must learn how to overcome them. For example, reporters learn early that you never use an ink pen when covering a fire. The spray from the fire hoses will wet the paper in your notebook and cause the ink to run. Use a pencil. Also, pens run out of ink; pencils don't. If the pencil point beaks, you can use your fingernail to peel back the wood and "re-sharpen" the pencil. The lesson: don't cut your fingernails too short; you may need them. Covering a speech? Where you sit is important. Size up the room. Where are the exits if you have to get out quickly? Where are the people sitting that you will need to talk to later? Which way will the speaker exit so you can get off a question when he walks by? It is important to anticipate things. Learning about such problems and dealing with them is an inherent part of the job. Effective journalists are observant, clever, innovative, and creative. It's rather like camping in the wilderness with nothing more than a pocketknife and learning how to survive.

• General Assignment •

For the general assignment (GA) reporter life is much less structured. The GA has no regular place to go each day to find news. Unlike the beat reporter who gets up and goes to his beat, the general assignment reporter must wander in search of things to write about. His day either begins with the editor assigning him something to cover or by finding some news on his own.

Either way, the general assignment reporter also knows it is important to pay attention to what's going on in the world. An event in a distant state or country might have an effect in his city. If people are launching a petition drive to eliminate smoking in bars in Indianapolis, is anyone thinking of doing it locally?

GA reporters must be more concerned with people and personality than with subject matter. The waitress who knows people by what they eat would make a good feature story. The man who builds an airplane in his basement only to find he can't get it out makes interesting reading. Consequently, the general assignment reporter is always on the lookout for the unusual, the dramatic.

The best general assignment reporters never sit in an office. While the beat reporter may feel tethered to a place so he can learn what's going on, the GA reporter wanders through the parks and alleyways, the crooks and crannies of the city for news. Not knowing what's going to happen next makes general assignment reporting exciting. You may be in New York covering an art exhibit opening one day, in the slums reporting on economic conditions of the poor the next, and interviewing a physicist about the future of space exploration in between. Obviously, whereas the beat reporter must be an expert in a particular area, the general assignment reporter must be a person of the world, knowledgeable about everything and ready to adapt to new situations at a moment's notice.

• Sources •

Regardless of where the journalist goes to get news, he will need sources — people and documents that provide the information for his stories. Remember, the journalist is most often reporting what others know. Obviously, the quality of the information he delivers will be determined by the quality of the information he uses, and that will reflect on his own ability as a journalist. Consequently, he must be very careful when it comes to the people he talks to and the documents he uses.

Journalists should always try to cultivate new sources and maintain old ones. With all the new technology, it would seem easier than ever to find and get sources, but ironically the Internet and telephone can often be an impediment to good reporting. Source material in whatever form begins with people. And getting out of the office and wearing down the shoe leather is still the best way to get and keep sources. People want to see you. If they can't see you, they can't know you, and if they don't know you, they won't trust you. And trust is paramount when trying to get information from others.

Sources include more than just "important" people. They include anyone who is in a position to know or to help find and verify information. Support staff, secretaries, librarians, and others are equally important because they can provide background information and help you find things. More than one source is essential to verify information, particularly if it is controversial. And in the end, the more sources you have, the more stories you'll get. They provide ideas for stories as well as the information for them.

Even when it comes to documents, human sources are imperative. They can help you understand and interpret reports, studies, and other written resources, which alone, can be foreign to everyone but the person who created them.

Good journalists must learn how to handle different sources. They are able to deal with different personalities. They can accommodate changes in moods and read body language. In addition to understanding the terms and procedures of their beats, they must be able to be human with people, to learn to commiserate, to compliment, without crossing the professional line between source and reporter. Remembering birthdays can go a long way to establishing rapport with people.

Also, not everything a journalist learns from a source is for publication or broadcast. The goal is not to embarrass people for no good reason. Journalists must learn to be discreet and tactful. They must understand that it is more important to watch and listen than to speak.

Credibility and accuracy are the two most important qualities reporters should look for when choosing a source. Primary sources are best. They have firsthand knowledge of the event or issue the journalist is investigating. They saw the car accident or did the study. Secondary sources, those who learned of the information secondhand, are next best. They include people who talked to people who were involved directly. These sources include lawyers representing others and police reports of what the victims said. In every case, the journalist is trying to get the source that is closest to the action or the primary document that explains the situation. He will always ask, who is in the best position to know? What is the authoritative study or document? Remember when you dropped a pebble into the water and how the waves made little circles that moved outward from the splash? You want to focus on the circle that's closest to the splash.

Sources also are identified in other ways. Named sources are called on-the-record sources or direct sources. Most stories come from direct sources. The information is always attributed, that is, identified as coming from the source. If the source is a person, he is identified by his name and title or some other way that indicates he is qualified to speak on the subject: *John Jones, a mechanic, said the engine had malfunctioned.* If the source is a document, then proper attribution of what the document is, where it came from, and who wrote it is required.

Background sources usually are not identified by name, though they may be identified by title or position, such as *a White House official said.* Using a background source may be the only way a journalist can get a particular story, but journalists should not overuse this technique because it prevents the reader, listener, or viewer from knowing who provided the information and, as a result, undermines the journalist's credibility and believability at a time when the credibility of journalism and journalists is low. Better to "train" public officials to expect to see their names in print.

Sometimes background sources literally provide background information that helps the reporter better understand the subject on which he is reporting. For example, a journalist may use reference sources and refer to his college physics text to help him understand specific terminology or theories or laws before he interviews a physicist. He may talk to the Undersecretary of the Navy about naval threats around the world before he goes in to interview the Secretary of the Navy about plans to build a new aircraft carrier. It will better help the journalist put questions in context of the global military situation and help him understand the rationale for the new carrier. These are useful sources that provide important information, but usually it's not information that directly explains the story on which he's working and so the source remains anonymous.

Generally, anonymous and confidential sources should be avoided. Again, they prevent the public from knowing who said what and call into question the credibility of the journalist. It causes people to ask if the journalist made up the story since they have no way of verifying it for themselves. This is becoming a growing problem as more people question the media.

As noted earlier, anonymous sources often provide background information and are usually identified in such a way as to indicate their position or occupation but not their name. Journalists use them far too often but sometimes argue that if they don't agree to keep a source's name out of the story, they won't get the story. Most of the time this gives too much power to the source over the story. Sometimes, using anonymous sources may be necessary, but the better practice is to try to avoid using them and working harder to get someone to comment on the record. Not getting the story is always a problem, but the bigger problem today is not being believed.

In addition to the ethical concerns associated with anonymous sources, use of confidential sources can cause legal problems. Therefore, only in rare situations should they be used — far less than they are used in the media today. Confidential sources, those whose name must be kept secret out of fear for their job or their life, should be used only after consulting an editor and perhaps an attorney. Even then, they must be used in a very specific way to avoid lawsuits.

The Journalist's Primer

Let's say a reporter has a source at the police department. He's a rookie cop. He comes to the reporter and tells him he has information that the chief is embezzling money, and that he'll tell the reporter about it if he keeps his name out of it. The reporter, hungry for a scoop (getting the story before someone else), agrees. Unfortunately for the reporter, he has just entered into a legally binding oral agreement.

Here's what can happen. The reporter, having given his word, gets the information from the cop and prints the story. The next thing he knows, the district attorney, who has read the story and has launched his own investigation into the police department, is calling him and asking where he got the information. The reporter tells him he can't reveal his confidential source. The district attorney informs him that he is withholding information of a possible crime. Still, the reporter, true to his word, refuses to answer. Suddenly, he is standing in front of a judge who is demanding to know where he got the information. He has a choice, the judge tells him; he can reveal his source or be found in contempt of court and go to jail where he will meet all manner of new and interesting people. Frightened, the reporter "burns" his source and reveals his name, thus avoiding jail. As a result, however, the rookie cop gets fired since everyone, including the police chief, now knows who the snitch is. The cop, angry about losing his job, gets a lawyer and sues the reporter (and the newspaper) for breach of contract. The cop wants $10 million — all the money he would have made during his career, plus health benefits, pension, etc., etc., etc. Will he get it? Probably, he will. The U.S. Supreme Court ruled 5-4 in 1991 in *Cohen v. Cowles Media Co.* (501 U.S. 663) that news sources can sue for breach of contract when the Press reveals their names after promising anonymity.

So how is one to use a confidential source? Most reporters and editors do not understand how to handle this question. The general advice is to tell the reporter to consult the editor, or try to better define or limit the terms of the agreement, or to get the source to go on the record. But these will not always avoid the possible legal problems.

Journalists have long argued that they should have a legal right called *privilege*, that is, they should be allowed to keep what is told to them secret the same way a lawyer or doctor can keep conversations between themselves and their clients and patients private. They say without this privilege many important stories that benefit the public will go unreported. But the courts have not recognized that privilege.

Some states have passed shield laws that require the police and other officials to try to get the information they need from others first. (An attempt to pass a federal shield law covering federal law is stalled in Congress.) But this only offers limited protection. In the end, if they can't get the information elsewhere, they can still come back to the reporter and make him reveal his source or face contempt.

The only way to avoid trouble, so far, is to not enter into the agreement with the source. That means not taking the information he offers and not offering him anonymity. Reporters don't like this plan because it means not getting the story — at least not easily.

Just because you can't get the information from the source, however, doesn't mean the source still can't be useful. For now, the safer way is to use the source as a *hinter*. Did you ever play *hot and cold* with your parents when you were young? They hid something and then told you if you were getting hot or cold the closer or farther away you got from it. The trick is to use the source the same way. Without allowing him to tell you anything, and thus likely avoiding a contract with him, have the source point you in the right direction so you can find it on your own or from another source willing to go on the record. Until the law is changed and privilege is granted, this may be the only way a reporter can use a confidential source somewhat safely.

An example of this technique is actually used in the movie *All the Presidents Men* detailing the Watergate scandal. In the movie, reporter Bob Woodward meets his confidential source in a parking garage in the middle of the night. The source tells Woodward to tell him what he knows about the story and that he will keep Woodward on the right track if he can. In the movie, the source refuses to give him the information. In real life, the reporter should refuse to take it.

The problem with this technique is that it may take the reporter days, months, or even years longer to get the story. He may not get it at all.

Journalists and sources often use different terms when it comes to attributing source material. Unfortunately, not all journalists and sources agree on the terms. They include *off the record, not for attribution, on background,* and *on deep background.* It's best to talk about and define these terms with sources before the talking starts.

The Journalist's Primer

Off the record means you can't use the information. The only exception to this rule is if you can get the information someplace else such as a public record or some other source or if it is already widely known. *Not for attribution* means you can use it but you can't attribute it to the source. *On background* means you can use it and reference it to a general, non-specific source such as *a White House official said*. *On deep background* generally means you can use the information but not name any source.

This can get confusing. Worse, sources can often begin talking and then announce that everything they just said is off the record. It's always best to have an understanding before talking to sources that you are a reporter and that unless agreed on in advance, everything is on the record. Otherwise, you're going to have to talk fast to convince them to put what they said back on the record.

Journalists should be aware of red flags when choosing a source, and they should ask themselves a host of questions to make sure the source is right for the story. They should ask, who is the source? What are his biases? Is the source capable of relating information accurately, objectively, or at least lucidly from his point of view? Does he have an ax to grind; is that why is he offering the information? Is he out to make someone look bad or get back at them? Is he qualified to comment? Is he in a position to know what he is talking about? What are his qualifications? Does he have any conflicts of interest? Again, the journalist must remember that the quality of his story will in large part be a reflection of the quality of his sources.

Journalists must also be on guard against being used or lied to. Public officials and politicians will often say things as trial balloons, mentioning some information without indicating where they stand on it just to see how the public reacts. The reporter writes about it, the public reacts one way or the other, and the politician learns about the public sentiment without giving away his position. At other times, people will, for all kinds of reasons, just lie. It's always best to verify the information by talking to more than just one source.

Lastly, never underestimate the value people who may not have the right title but nevertheless are in a position to know. Years ago, I knew a shoeshine man who worked on a street corner in the banking district of Orlando, Florida. Every week I would go down and talk to him and get my shoes shined and listen as he explained what was going on in the financial community of one of the larger cities in the state. I was shocked by the extent of his knowledge and understanding. I asked how he knew so much, and he told me that he was in a unique position to get information. He said every afternoon bank leaders would show up to have their shoes shined, and he would listen as they talked about what was going on in their world. He paid attention, invested his money accordingly, and got rich. I asked why he just didn't quit and retire. He gave me a sly smile and asked me why he would ever walk away from a place that made him so much money.

We grew to trust one another, and soon he was telling me what they were telling him. I agreed to keep our relationship confidential. It drove the bankers nuts when I confronted them with the latest developments going on in their own banks. They must have turned their institutions inside out trying to find out who was leaking such privileged information, never realizing they were doing it themselves.

• The Morgue and Online Searches •

No, we're not talking about dead people here; we're talking about dead stories. The morgue is the newspaper's library or archive. Previously published stories are often the first place journalists look when working on a new story. They want to see what else has already been written about the subject. If the reporter is working on a story about a bank president receiving an award and the president has already been in another story, the reporter can get lots of useful background information from the first story. He must verify that it's correct, of course, but it tells him what else has been newsworthy about the man as well as how to spell his name, other sources he can contact about him, and additional information he might be able to use.

After searching the morgue, the next step is to look elsewhere online. Search engines such as Google as well as government and commercial databases and other news sites offer a wealth of information. But be careful, it is important that journalists check the credibility of online sources just as they would any other source. Generally speaking, academic, news, and government sources are more credible than commercial ones, but all of them must undergo the same scrutiny for accuracy, verification from other sources, bias, and context. It is important also to check how old the information is. It may be out of date and therefore inaccurate. Regardless of where you get information, it is still imperative that you attribute it. Beware also of copyright laws. Using too much protected material without permission can get you into legal trouble.

Finally, don't forget the old standbys for information: the phone book, city directories, cross references, maps, government directories, the Congressional Record, the dictionary and almanac, among others. Half of any journalist's job is to know where to go to get information. The prudent reporter is always on the lookout for new sources of information.

• News Releases •

Another source of information is the public relations or press release. New products and discoveries and innovations come from the business community every day. If it weren't for the public relations industry, a lot of news in business, medicine, technology, and just about every other area of commerce, would never get reported. There simply aren't enough reporters in the world to cover everything.

News releases can come by mail, by email, over the Internet, or by social media. But however they come they should be researched and written the same way as any news story, with tight writing and factual reporting.

The difference, of course, between a news story and a PR release is that people who write PR releases are employed to promote a business or product, individual, or service. Most news releases, therefore, are often one-sided or slanted in favor of the organization or person that distributed them. Sometimes the information in them is false or filled with half-truths. More often, they simply emphasize the facts that put their point of view in the best light, often ignoring or downplaying those facts or attitudes that are critical or contradictory or provide context. Put another way, they will frame the story to their liking. For example, if a produce company is in the news because dangerous bacteria in its lettuce has been making people sick, the company's PR people will send out releases announcing what the company is doing right to make the product safe. The news, of course, is about the contamination — that's the change in the status quo that made it news to begin with — not that the company is doing something right, which they're supposed to be doing anyway. Obviously, if everything were okay there would be no news in the first place. For this reason, journalists should use PR releases only as a starting point for a story and never as an end product to be printed verbatim.

Remember, the role of a journalist is not to promote; it is to inform the reader, listener, and viewer of all sides of the story without taking sides. That means the information in any press release, including the spelling of names, must be verified and other questions should be asked to get all sides of the story. This means you will need to contact people other than just the person who wrote or submitted the release and others besides those quoted or noted in the release. Ask yourself what information is missing, or what other contrary positions should be explored. As you investigate further, you may find that the focus of the release changes. A minor point may become the bigger story.

Other releases may simply announce that something is going to happen on a certain date. As a result, journalists should pay attention to and try to honor the PR release date noted at the top of most releases. To announce the information prematurely may mean getting the story wrong. Most releases note that the information is for immediate release, but not all do.

The bottom line is to be careful with information that comes from people whose goal is promotion first and information second.

• Exercise •

Have each student select a news story topic and make a list of potential sources for that story.

• Techniques •

Ultimately, news is about people. Consequently, one cannot be an effective information gatherer without also being an effective interviewer. Sooner or later you've got to be able to talk to someone — and persuade that person to talk back to you.

Interviewing is not a science, and it's more than a skill; it's an art, and the very best journalists are always at the top of their game during the interview, able to get to the heart of a person and show us who he really is. To do this, the effective journalist must do more than just get the other person to answer questions; he must establish a rapport that puts the other person at ease and makes him open up and be himself. As a result, the journalist is able to see the person more fully and that adds depth and humanity to his reporting. It also enables the audience to understand the person and his answers better.

The Journalist's Primer

No one can teach you to be a great interviewer. Much of it has to do with each reporter's personality. Some people have the knack; others don't. Most of the time, those who have learned to do it well have learned through practice. To make things more difficult, what works in one interview with one person will not necessarily work in another interview with another person, though many of the techniques are the same.

Interviewing is like riding a horse. The rider must not only know where he is going and give clear directions, but he must also pay attention to his surroundings and look for the little signs that indicate changes in the horse's attitude and mood. He has to know when to take charge and pull back on the reins and when to loosen his grip on the reins and give the horse its head. The interviewer must pay attention to more than just the questions and the answers. He has to be aware of everything that may affect the conversation and work it to make that conversation productive.

Interviews may last several hours or be conducted over several days, weeks, months, or even years, or they may take as long as it takes for a person to walk down the courthouse steps and get into a car. In any case, all interviews start much the same way — with research. Each journalist should know as much as possible about the topic and the individual he is going to interview before he begins asking questions. He should know more than the interviewee thinks he knows — always — because the more the interviewer knows, the better able he will be to determine when the interviewee is lying or speaking in half-truths. The amount of research one does often will be determined by the complexity of the topic or by the amount of time the journalist has to prepare.

For example, let's say the journalist is going to interview a bank president who has just won a banker of the year award. This isn't a breaking police story that requires the journalist to speed to the scene of an accident. He has some time.

His first action likely will be to call to set up an interview. The time and place are important. Non-threatening interviews involving "good" news, such as this one, or where the interviewee is shy or reluctant to talk, are usually best conducted where the subject feels most comfortable, in natural surroundings. That not only helps put the interviewee at ease and prompt him to be more open during the conversation, it also allows the interviewer to gain a better sense of who he is by seeing his surroundings. Pictures on the wall and desk, mementos on the bookshelves, all of these give insight into the person.

If, on the other hand, the interview will likely involve hard, pointed questions regarding some potential wrongdoing that causes the interviewee to become defensive, it's best to try to conduct the interview in some neutral location where the interviewee won't be able to sit in his big chair behind his big desk in a position of superiority while the interviewer sinks down into a side chair with his eyes below desk level feeling cowed and weak. (If this is not possible, sit up straight on the edge of the chair.) All interviews are best conducted with the parties seeing eyeball to eyeball. Journalists should not assume a position of superiority, nor should they feel lesser than their subjects — even if it's the president of the United States. The idea is to conduct a conversation that encourages each person to be open and honest and equally human. If you feel intimidated or superior or treat them as a fan, you won't be able to do a good job.

After the journalist has set up the interview, the next step is to check the news library for past stories about the banker. This will give the reporter basic information — everything from how to spell his name to his age and where he went to school. It should also provide the journalist with other sources — friends, colleagues, and perhaps even those who disagree with him on certain issues. The journalist will check with each of these sources. Each will require a separate interview. He will also go online to find other information and other sources. Obviously, he will want to know something about the award itself. More research. The journalist should understand which sources are necessary and which are not and what each source will add to the story. For example, friends can give insight into his personality. Family can tell us about his childhood. Colleagues can tell us about the way he works. Enemies can illuminate weaknesses. Each interview he conducts should add to his knowledge about his subject. When do we quit looking for information and sources? We quit when we exhaust all the questions concerning the topic. And when do we know when that happens? A good rule of thumb is to quit when you start getting the same information again and again from different sources.

Before the journalist conducts each interview, and especially before he conducts the interview with people like the banker, the journalist will need to make a list of questions. Which questions he asks will be determined by what information he seeks. For example, the questions for the banker will center on the banker receiving the award — the reason for the interview in the first place. Since all stories must answer who, what, when, where, how, and why, a good place to begin is with those questions. I call them *extending the questions*. In other words, start with the *who* and ask all the *who* questions you can think of. Who are you? Who gave you the award? Who helped you get the award? Who else has received the award? Etc., etc., etc. Then go on and ask all the *what* questions you can think of, and so on. When the journalist is finished, he should have a good group of core questions relating to the topic. Finally, he should ask himself, is there anything else I should ask that I haven't asked?

The next step is to divide the questions into three groups — those questions involving short answers, such as name, age, address, etc., those questions involving medium length answers, where the bulk of the interview will take place, and those questions involving long or embarrassing answers — which are usually saved for last.

In most cases the reason for this organization is obvious. First, many, if not most, of the short answer questions could be answered before the interview, thus saving lots of time for other questions. Most people are busy, especially important people, and making the most of limited time is essential. Doing the homework about their background from other documents and sources can glean important information. It's easier to ask the banker's secretary to fax you the banker's bio than to waste his time asking basic questions during the interview, questions that would make the reporter appear stupid and inept. Finally, we save the questions involving long or embarrassing answers for last to either cleverly extend the interview time or to prevent the interview from being a complete bust because the interviewee got mad and threw the journalist out of the room.

The journalist should have built up a rapport with the interviewee by the end of the interview. The interviewee should feel comfortable by then and, if the interviewer works it right, he can ask long questions that involve more time to answer, and the interviewee, now comfortable talking about subjects he knows, will take the extra time to answer. This clever trick can often turn a half hour interview into an hour or longer. If the question involves an embarrassing answer, and the interviewee gets mad and ends the interview, the bulk of the interview is already finished. The loss of a question won't hurt the story. If the journalist asks the pointed question right up front and gets booted, he leaves with nothing.

This formula will not work in every interview situation. If the journalist is limited by time, he will need to get right to the point. Sometimes an entire story hinges on the answer to one or two questions. "Did you do it?" may be the only real question as the accused is rushed into the police station. His answer will be the focus of the story. The rest of it will be background information about the crime. In those situations, the journalist must go through his prepared questions and figure out the ones, in order of importance, that he must get answered. Often, you only get a few moments — perhaps long enough to ask one or two questions before the door is slammed in your face.

If you have time, you should number and type each question. Then when you ask the question, you can write down the number of the question and the interviewee's answer next to it on a separate sheet of paper. This way if an answer goes on for a long time, you're not trying to squeeze your writing on the same page on which you wrote your questions.

Draw a line across the page separating each answer. And put the name, title, cell phone number, and email address for each person you interview at the top of the first page of the set of questions you ask them.

If you know shorthand, use it. If not, you will need to develop your own kind of shorthand. People talk fast and quotes must be verbatim. Although you will paraphrase most information your source gives you, quotes are important to include in the story because they characterize the speaker as well as give information. That adds personality and interest. For example, you could paraphrase Admiral Farragut's famous Civil War order and say he didn't particularly care about the mines in the harbor and ordered his ships forward anyway, or you could use his familiar quote and write "Damn the torpedoes," full speed ahead. Obviously, the second method adds something to the story that the paraphrase does not.

Listen for quotes that are short (they're easier to get right) and that capture the theme or essence of what the person is saying. Broadcasters call these *sound bites*. In essence, they are a few words that summarize everything the speaker has been talking about.

If the story is complex or you think the subject may recant what he said later, record the conversation. If the person doesn't want to be recorded, remind him that you don't want to misquote him. Don't ask if you can do it; just do it. You wouldn't ask if you could use a pencil and paper. It's a tool of the trade. If, on the other hand, the person becomes self-conscious and clams up, making it difficult to get anything, casually reach over and turn off the recorder, and make sure the interviewee sees you do it. Never rely on the recorder alone. Too often, they break and you're left with nothing but a fuzzy memory. Also, you may not have time to go back and transcribe your notes from the recorder. Use the recorder as a backup only to double-check your notes for accuracy.

Generally, it's a bad idea to record conversations secretly. Depending upon how and where you do it, it may be illegal. In most states, the law requires that at least one person to the conversation be aware that the conversation is being recorded. Since the reporter knows he's recording his own conversation that qualifies. But some states require that all people to the conversation be made aware.

One of the more vexing problems is how to handle the *split interview*. (My term.) This will take your juggling skills to a whole new level. Let's say you are interviewing the bank president and during the interview he mentions that he is going to bring a professional football team to the city. This is major news. And it just made your interview more difficult.

Now instead of one story, you suddenly have two. If he drops other news, you have even more stories. The question is how to handle them, and it's a question you've got to answer in about five or ten seconds. Unfortunately, several other questions must be answered first, and even more quickly. How long is the interview? What are my chances of extending it, of getting the subject to talk about the other story, of having him get mad and cancel the one he's agreed to do? If you think you can pull it off, you've got to ask yourself next how you can pursue both stories at the same time. Do I ask all my questions about one story and then ask questions about the new one? And If I do that, what happens if he is interrupted and has to cut the interview short before I can get into the new story? Do I interrupt my line of questioning on the story I agreed to do and then come back to it later after I've asked about the new one? How do I keep questions and answers for both stories separate so I don't get the stories mixed up? It can be a mess.

The general rule is to always get what news you can, but especially the story you asked for to begin with. And it's always best at least to try to answer the basic questions of who, what, when, where, how, and why of every story dropped on you. Depending upon your time and how willing the person is to endure further prodding, try to get whatever else you can.

The least obtrusive method is probably to ask all the basic questions then return to your original story and work in questions about the new story as you proceed through the originally planned interview. Again separate the answers with a line, but place a symbol or something beside each question and answer that is related to the new story he just revealed. As I said, this can get quite complicated if the interviewee keeps dropping news flashes.

If you need more time during questions, a useful delaying tactic is to ask the subject to explain what he means. Even though you may understand, it gives you time to write while he's talking. It's okay to not understand and ask him to repeat or try to explain it another way. Remember, the worst thing you can do is get it wrong. Don't be afraid to ask follow up questions. Sometimes even more important information will come from him as he collects his thoughts and answers another way or elaborates on an earlier comment.

Other situations require different tactics. Suppose the story is not about a bank president, but a bank robbery. The journalist does not have time to leisurely research the story. He has to move and move fast.

If a photographer and a reporter are assigned the story — a luxury in today's converged media world where one person is supposed to do it all — the photographer drives to the scene while the journalist figures out who he needs to talk to and what he needs to ask, making notes in his notebook. If he's a one-man show, he will need to drive and think at the same time. (Try not to drive and write at the same time.)

Since the situation is about a bank robbery, the focus of the story is clear and so too the people he needs to talk to. The people at a bank robbery who may know something might include witnesses, the bank teller, the bank robber, the bank president, the security guard, the police, and the F.B.I. As noted earlier, the journalist wants to talk to those who are closest to the action and work his way outward since those closest will know the most.

Unfortunately, in today's image-conscious world, this is getting ever harder to do as police tape off crime areas and public relations representatives sweep in and sequester employees from the Press while demanding that all information come through them. This control allows them to pasteurize and homogenize the information to make the bank look good while offering few details about the crime.

The Journalist's Primer

To combat this tendency, it is important that reporters first cultivate a wide range of sources in all levels of society, including banks, and second get to the scene quickly and speak to those closest to the action who may leave or be hustled off by authorities or others. Obviously, those individuals would include witnesses and the bank teller. Chances are the robber is gone, dead, or caught. Next in line would be the bank security guard and then the bank president. Police come next; F.B.I agents come last. Effective journalists know to hang around but not bother the police while they are investigating. They just got there themselves and chances are they know little more than the journalist. But stay close and watch, waiting for the opportune moment to ask questions.

Despite the chaos and activity, try to remain calm and thoughtful. Watch and see what's really going on. Often while other journalists are running around in a pack, you can get the bigger story by going your own way. I got one of the better stories of my career by ignoring the herd and following my own instincts during a deportation hearing of an accused Nazi. While everyone else ran after the obvious sources and all got the same information, I found out where the guy lived and went and talked to his neighbors. Everybody else got the basic story; I got the exclusive.

Question formation even in this situation is much the same. Extend the basic questions of who, what, when, where, how, and why with regard to things each source will be able to talk about. For example, when talking to the teller ask who he is, who was the bank robber, who is your boss, who were the witnesses, etc. Some of the questions will overlap: When did it happen, what time did it happen? That's OK. You can always go back and edit out the redundancies. Better to ask too many questions than not enough.

In any situation, observe good manners and the social customs of where you are. If you are in an office setting, manners are more formal than if you are at a ball game. If you are in Saudi Arabia, they will be quite different indeed. Know the culture. Generally, don't sit down until asked to do so. Don't chew gum. Don't assume familiarity with the interviewee before it's established. Be considerate of secretaries and others. They have more power than you think. Be careful what you say outside of the interview process. Others are listening. Be quietly confident. Know why you're there and what you've come for. It's your interview. Maintain eye contact. Timidity can be as crippling in an interview as over-familiarity.

Most of the time, professional dress is preferred. If you can adapt, do so. For example, don't show up to the White House in jeans and don't go to a rodeo in a suit. Dress for the situation. It makes you and the interviewee more comfortable and encourages relaxed conversation. Never dress in such a way as to draw attention to yourself. No loud clothes or too much jewelry or makeup. If you have a tattoo, cover it. If you don't have one, don't get one. Regardless of what you think about them, they get in the way. You are there to get people to talk, but not about you.

Everything matters in an interview. And you, as the interviewer, must be aware of everything. Like a juggler with eight balls in the air, you have to keep track of all of them at the same time. Watch and pay attention to what the interviewee says, how he acts, as well as what he doesn't say. Unspoken communication can say a lot. If the person is shy or nervous or unresponsive, ask open-ended questions that can't be answered with a yes or no answer. Instead of how was your day, ask them to describe their day. If, on the other hand, the interviewee is in love with his own words and won't stop talking, asked closed ended questions instead. The job is to keep the conversation going without dominating it.

If you are nervous, take a few breaths or imagine the person you are about to interview in a humble position that brings him down to earth and makes him human. Imagine him working in the garden or cleaning the toilet. If he is nervous, put him at ease with some small talk or ask him a question about some item in the office. If he is hostile or hurried, be polite, but get down to business. Always have your opening line ready. Know how you're going to open and close.

Sometimes it's helpful to test the waters, to ask a pointed question during the interview and then back off and let them cool down while asking something less confrontational. Timing is important. It's vital that you gain a feeling for the conversation and the person you are talking to. You must know when you can push the envelope and when you can't, when the conversation is straying or the person is being evasive. Sometimes it's helpful to give away certain information to let them know that you know. At other times, you never want to tip your hand so you can keep them on guard. Remember that patience is a virtue. Don't be tempted to talk when there is a question on the table. Be quiet. Let the pregnant pause drag on. Let them get antsy and do the talking. Know that every interview is unique and this is not an exact science. You'll have to figure it out as you go.

Smile (unless you're covering a tragedy). Don't be afraid to be human, to put yourself in the other person's place. It's okay to tell them a little about yourself if the situation calls for it. People tend to open up and respond in kind. For the interviewee, reporters are sometimes a substitute for therapists. But don't overdo it and never take gifts. Don't tell people you know how they feel; you don't.

Generally speaking, interviews should never be conducted at a bar over drinks. It's too easy for people to recant what they told you and claim they didn't know what they were saying because of the booze. If you take them to a restaurant or out to coffee, pick up the tab. This is a way to be gracious and thank them for their time. It also eliminates the feeling of indebtedness and the appearance that they are paying you off.

As the interview is concluding, ask yourself if you have left anything out, if there is question you should have asked, but didn't, and ask the interviewee if he would like to add anything. Ask where he will be later and how you can get in touch with him if you have additional questions or want to clarify something. If he balks or is hesitant, tell him you want to make sure you get the story right. More than likely he'll want you to get it right also and give you the contact information. Then thank him for his time. Always. Even if he's rude.

What happens next is critical. If it's not a breaking story and you have some time, find the nearest restroom, go inside, and enter an empty stall. Take out your notebook, sit on the commode and go over your notes. Most of us write quickly during an interview to get it all down. If you leave the interview and don't review your notes right away, you won't be able to figure out what you wrote by the time you get back to the office or even to your car. Go over each sentence and print the difficult to read words clearly above the scribble. This can also have added benefits. Often after an interview, the subject will also go to the restroom and talk about what he just endured. It's amazing what else you can learn — about the topic and yourself. Follow-up questions may be in order.

• Defining the Story •

Whether a journalist works as a beat reporter or a general assignment reporter, whether he gets information from a person or a document, the steps to researching a story are much the same. After all the research has been done and the information gathered, the journalist must make sense of what he's got. He must find what journalists call the *peg*. Put simply, it's what the story is about, the reason it exists.

Sometimes, it's easy. For example, if we are going to cover a car accident, the story is obviously about a car accident — the event determines the news.

But not all stories are so easily identified. Sometimes stories emerge only after we have uncovered lots of seemingly unrelated facts. Slowly we begin to see a picture or theme emerge of what the story is really about. The facts all begin to point toward a general premise. For example, a reporter covers what appears to be a simple burglary and as he continues to research he realizes the story is about political intrigue and criminal activity in the highest office in the land — a story that began just that way and is known today as Watergate. It is always important that the journalist let the facts determine the story and not rush to some preconceived idea of what he thinks the story is about. Nor must he base his determination on just a few facts. The job of the journalist is to pull the thread, and keep pulling, until he sees where it goes.

This doesn't mean that the journalist begins with no idea at all about the story. Everything begins with a working premise — even the most stringent, academic, scientific research begins with a working hypothesis. It just means that the reporter should not be locked into his idea of what the story is about; the facts may change the direction of the story. Consequently, all journalists start with the facts presented to them and work outward until they have exhausted all their questions. Only then can they figure out what they've really got. Ultimately, this is what defines the story.

For example, if we hear about a commotion downtown and go to investigate and find that two cars collided, we start with a *what* and a working hypothesis that we're covering a car accident. The more facts we gather about the event, the better we're able to understand if we're on the right track. But as new facts emerge, we may discover that the driver of one of the cars is a famous celebrity. Now the story is not just about a *what* but also a *who*. Which is more important and which defines the story depends on just how big the accident is or how famous the celebrity is.

The Journalist's Primer

As we noted earlier then, context is equally important in helping us define the story. Good journalists always gather many more facts than they need or will use to tell their story. This helps them determine the boundaries of the story — that is, which facts to include in the story so it can be told accurately and completely and which to leave out.

Think of it this way. Let's say we're again covering the auto accident. We go and we start asking anyone who might know something about the event — the car accident — about what happened. As a result, we find out who was involved, when it happened, where it happened, how it happened, and why it happened. As we seek out these answers, we will undoubtedly learn other facts. For example, we may learn that it was a sunny day, that the investigating police officer's middle name is Earl, that a dog was barking at the police officer, and that the driver who was ticketed for running a stop sign and causing the crash has a mother in the hospital. All of these facts appear to have no bearing on our ability to understand the story — the defining reason why facts are included in any story. Our inclination, therefore, is to leave them out.

But, let's say that as we investigate further, we learn that the ticketed driver had just found out that his mother had suffered a heart attack and that he was rushing to the hospital to see her at the time of the collision. Now the story takes on added meaning and understanding — perhaps he was distracted by the bad news and that was a reason for running the stop sign. We obviously can't speculate, but we now know other questions to ask to get to the bottom of what really happened and why — none of which we would have learned had we not dug deeper for more facts. Now, the seemingly unrelated fact that the driver had a mother in the hospital is important to the story. Without digging deep for the story, the journalist has no idea what the story really might be about. Only by being curious, by wanting to know everything he can about what is happening and exhausting all possible questions will he understand which facts to leave in the story and which to take out. And only this way will he be able to tell the real story.

• Exercise •

Have students interview one another and see which student can find the most information within forty-five minutes.

CHAPTER

7

Writing the News for Print

• Prewriting •

When first trying to write the story, journalists always ask themselves a simple question: "What is my story about?" Regardless of your topic, if you can't answer that question, you're not ready to write. Furthermore, the answer should come in one simple sentence. My story is about …

It doesn't matter if you're writing a news story, a screenplay, a short story, or a novel, all writers must be able to answer that question simply and directly. Editors will often ask reporters this question when they return from gathering information. Some will help you figure it out; others will tell you to go to your desk to think about it some more. If you can't answer the question, it's often because you haven't done enough research or because you don't understand the research you've done. Or you've failed to see the common thread that runs through the research.

If you're stuck, first go back and check to see that you've answered the six questions of who, what, when, where, how, and why. No story is complete unless and until all of them are addressed. If you're still having trouble, try asking yourself what is your most interesting fact, your most exciting fact, or your most important fact. Or you may try finding the verb that describes what's going on. If you were covering a fire, you would look to words like damaged, destroyed, burned, etc., to tell your story.

Sometimes the best way to figure it out is to spread your notes out in front of you and let them tell the story back to you. Ask yourself, what am I trying to say, what is most important in all these facts, and what is the best way to get it across to others.

One method writers use is the "Hey, Mom!" approach. Remember when you were a child and something happened and you ran home, rushed in the door and yelled "Hey, Mom! Guess what?" and then you proceeded to tell her the news? Imagine yourself in that situation. If you had to rush in the front door and yell that to your mother, what would you say? What's the point of your story?

Once you have determined what your story is about, you're ready to organize the facts in such a way that you can explain the story to others.

• The Inverted Pyramid •

Remember that content always determines form. It's never the other way around. We don't say I'm now going to write a feature story when the facts before us indicate we have a news story; we look to the facts to tell us what kind of story we've got — news, feature, investigative, whatever — and then write the kind of story the facts indicate. Or we find the facts that support a particular kind of story we want to write. If we want to write a feature story, we look for the kind of information that lends itself to that kind of story. In any case, all stories have structures — a way to organize and present the information.

The print news story structure resembles an inverted pyramid. That's because it looks like an upside down pyramid with the wide base at the top and the point at the bottom. The wide parts of the pyramid signify the more important information in the story. Consequently, since the widest part of the pyramid — the base — is at the top, we know that the most crucial information needed to understand the story comes first. That's where we find the who, what, when, where, how, and why questions answered — the essential questions in any story. As we read down through the story, we note that the pyramid gets narrower until we get to the bottom and the point. This means that as we read down through the story the information becomes less important and necessary to our understanding.

There are several historical and psychological reasons for this structure. Two hundred years ago, writers used flowery prose. Their writing included lots of adjectives and adverbs and convoluted sentence structures that added to the length of stories. As newspaper printing costs increased, publishers needed their reporters to tell stories more efficiently and succinctly — i.e., more information in less space. They found that by using an inverted pyramid structure and putting the most important information at the top of each story, they could fit more news in the paper.

Think of it this way. Editors decide what news will go into each day's newspaper. And then they lay out the paper. That is, they figure out where the different stories go on each page. Each story on each page is allotted a particular spot with a set amount of space. This space is measured in column inches — the width of a newspaper column by so many inches long. More important stories are given more space.

Let's say you wrote a story about the mayor proposing a new park and the editor assigned you six inches for the story. That means you must tell that story in six column inches to fit the space assigned in the newspaper. Now let's say you wrote the story in eight inches. Obviously, an eight-inch story will not fit into a six-inch space. So to make the story fit, the editor simply cuts off the bottom two inches. Now the story fits. If you have written the story according to the inverted pyramid with the most important information at the top and the least important information at the bottom, the reader will be denied only the least important information. If you've answered the main questions of who, what, when, where, how, and why at the top, the reader still gets the gist of the story. Technically, you should be able to cut a story from the bottom all the way up to the first paragraph and still have the story make sense.

Nevertheless, editors must be careful that they don't cut information that's critical to keeping the story in context. Short of that, the reader still gets the news, albeit less of it.

The Journalist's Primer

Reporters learned this in the field, too, with the advent of the telegraph. Telegraph operators charge for each word they send. Consequently, journalists learned that they needed to use few words and get to the point of each story quickly. If they answered the six questions early, they at least got the news out.

This system also plays well in our busy lives. Readers don't want to wade through a lot of prose to get to the point of any story. Putting the news first allows them to find out what each story is about quickly. If they want more information, they can read further. Technically, you should be able to scan the first couple of paragraphs of every news story in the paper and get a summary of the days news.

Story structure isn't the only thing reporters must consider. The denotation and connotation of words, grammar, spelling, punctuation, style, and sentence structure are all important, too. Consider the following sentences. *I shall drown; no one will save me!* and *I will drown; no one shall save me!* Do they mean the same thing? All we did was switch two words. No. In one scenario we're dealing with an attempted suicide; in the other, we're dealing with an accident. Which is which? Does it matter? It does if you're trying to save them or even if you're trying to explain the event to others. When he says in the first sentence that he shall drown, he is saying he is determined to drown, since shall is first person determinative, and that no one will — statement of fact — save him. While in the second situation, he has come to the realization that it's a fact he's going to drown because no one is determined to come and save him.

Journalists often forget that they are writing history and that people a thousand years from now will read what they wrote and watch and listen to what they recorded to figure out what happened. Get it wrong and the past remains a mystery to them.

Given the need to tell stories clearly and succinctly, journalists write simple declarative sentences, using simple words, focusing on concrete nouns and action verbs, and keeping subjects and verbs close together near the front of each sentence: *John hit the ball.* And they say something new in each sentence. (The better writers can say several things in each sentence without using a bunch of words.) They also tend to avoid adjectives, and if they see an adverb, they kill it. Adverbs are the words that tell how something was done, which usually means they are the commentary of the writer — a journalistic no-

no when it comes to objective reporting. Simple writing is the best writing. Remember, you're not writing to make yourself seem important by using a bunch of big words. Write to express, not to impress. You want writing that is clear, concise, complete, and compelling — the four c's.

How you format your story may vary from newsroom to newsroom in this computer age, but generally, the default hard-copy (on paper) approach is to start with the *slug* — one or two words identifying the subject of the story — on the first line in the upper left hand corner of the paper. Place your name on the second line beneath the slug and put the date on the line beneath your name. On the fourth line note whether any photograph, map, accompanying sidebar, etc., goes with the story by writing *with photo* etc. Next, skip one third of the way down the page and begin writing your story, indenting paragraphs and double-spacing the lines. Keep the paragraphs short. When you have finished the story, double-space and write *30*, which means the end in journalism parlance.

• Leads •

The inverted pyramid structure with important information at the top and less important information later often resembles the classic structure of a typical paragraph. Think back to junior high English class. Remember when the teacher told you a paragraph contained a topic sentence followed by supporting sentences? The topic sentence defined what the paragraph was going to address and the supporting sentences provided the facts that, well, supported the topic. It's much the same with the classic print news story. We move from general information — the basic gist of the story, to the specifics — the supporting details. In the beginning paragraph, therefore, we would say the robbery happened Tuesday — the general time — and wait until the body to note the specific time — 2 a.m.

Consequently, the inverted pyramid is itself divided into two parts — the lead (or lede) and the body. The lead is the first paragraph where we get the general information about the story, the gist, and the body is where we get the specific facts that support the premise of the story that's in the lead. Of the two, lead and body, the lead is the more important.

That's because leads do a lot of things, all of them critical to the story. They define the story for the reader; that is, they tell the reader the theme of the story, what journalists call the "peg." Remember, it's the idea the story hangs on or what the story is about. They also generally sum up the story by answering most or all of the six questions relating to the peg. They set the tone. And by noting what the story is about, they help the journalist determine how the rest of the story unfolds or is structured. Consequently, if the reporter gets the lead wrong, chances are the rest of the story is out of order in terms of what is important. Given the importance of the lead, therefore, many reporters will spend most of their time writing the lead. In fact, it's not uncommon for a reporter, if he has an hour to write a story, to spend 40 minutes on the lead and write the rest of the entire story in the last 20 minutes.

Most journalists work with four different kinds of leads and try to avoid a fifth one. Which one they use depends on the kind of story they are doing.

The first one is the summary lead, which, as expected, summarizes the who, what, when, where, how, and why of the story in one paragraph. The problem with this is that it often becomes long and cumbersome and difficult to read. For example:

> *John Jones, 82, of 418 E. Maple St., a retired auto mechanic, was killed in a four-car accident Thursday at Broadway and Second Streets when police said the brakes failed on his pickup truck and he ran a red light.*

In an effort to shorten the lead and get the reader into the story more quickly, reporters often use a variation of the summary lead called the delayed-identification lead. For example:

> *An 82-year-old retired auto mechanic was killed in a four-car accident Thursday at Broadway and Second Streets when police said the brakes failed on his pickup truck and he ran a red light. John Jones, 82, of 418 E. Maple St., was taken to Mercy Hospital following the 2 p.m. crash but died of internal injuries, family members said.*

By delaying the identity of the who of the story until the second paragraph, the writer is able to entice the reader to move further into the story to see who the story is about. The theory is that the more time a reader spends with a story, the more likely it is that he will continue reading it.

The third kind of lead is called a blind lead. Blind leads are used more often in feature stories. They don't summarize anything. Instead they are written to grab the reader's attention with some fact that peaks his interest and pulls him into the story.

> *Bill Rand woke up Thursday with a million dollars and a headache.*

The reader is interested because he wants to know why anyone who just got a million dollars would have a headache.

A fourth kind of lead is the second-day lead or follow-up lead. This lead is used when the journalist is reporting on a new development in a previously reported story. For example, the first story might be about a man who fell out of a boat but whose body has not yet been found. The second-day story would be about authorities searching for his body.

> *The search will continue Thursday for the body of a local man who is believed to have drowned Wednesday in Stanley Lake after falling from a boat.*

Notice that the lead starts with the latest news or development in the story first.

The last lead is one the reporter never wants to write. It's called a "wooden" lead. Sometimes editors refer to them as "speaker speaks" leads. The problem is that they are so general that they say nothing. For example:

> *The Rev. John Jones spoke about UFOs Sunday at the First Baptist Church.*

It purports to be a summary lead, but it's so vague that it's useless. What did he say about them? Technically, a lead that is designed to give us news should do just that. It should be complete enough that we can stop reading the story after the first paragraph and still have gotten the essential information.

The Journalist's Primer

Remember, before a reporter can write his story he must understand what it is about. He must be able to sum it up in one sentence. My story is about... This is the first essential step to writing that first paragraph since the lead tells the reader what the topic is.

Most stories are about who or what. Rarely are they about when or where. Occasionally they may be about why or how. But whatever the focus, the easiest way to start the paragraph is by figuring out what the story is about and putting that first in the lead.

For example, let's say a reporter rushed to an event in the city and came away with the following facts.

Who	-	two people injured
What	-	fire
When	-	Tuesday
Where	-	downtown Oklahoma City restaurant
How	-	hot grease spilled on some curtains
Why	-	waiter said he tripped and spilled the grease

Let's also say the reporter found out that the fire caused $1 million in damages.

By looking at the facts, we see that the story is about a fire. It's certainly not about Tuesday. The fire is the most important fact, the most interesting. It drives the story. If you used the "Hey, Mom!" approach, you would probably get right to the point by yelling "Hey, Mom!" Guess What? There's a big fire..." People are impatient. They don't want to wait until the end of the sentence to find out the big news. Consequently, we put it first.

So now we're ready to begin writing our lead.

A fire...

What's next? Well, we need a verb. What did the fire do? We see from the facts that it injured two people and caused $1 million in damages. Given the other facts, these two facts appear to be more important and interesting. So we put them next.

A fire injured two people and caused $1 million in damages...

Now what? By now the sentence should start to unfold on its own logically. We would want to know when and where.

> *A fire injured two people and caused $1 million in damages Tuesday at a downtown Oklahoma City restaurant...*

Often how and why come last because they take longer to answer. Sometimes it's so difficult to answer them that we put them in the following paragraph or paragraphs. Consequently, we usually put them last in the sentence. Also, logically it usually makes more sense to tell what happened before explaining why and how it happened.

> *A fire injured two people and caused $1 million in damages Tuesday at a downtown Oklahoma City restaurant after a waiter said he tripped and spilled hot grease on some curtains.*

Now we have our lead. It answers all six questions and sums up the story. The only thing left is the attribution — who gave us the information.

> *A fire injured two people and caused $1 million in damages Tuesday at a downtown Oklahoma City restaurant after a waiter said he tripped and spilled hot grease on some curtains, firefighters said.*

This does not mean you're through working on it, however. What we've done is use the default method of writing a lead by putting what the story is about first in the sentence and then working to fill in the rest. Effective writers will want to play with the sentence structure to see if they can improve it. So what other ways are there to write the lead?

"Caused" is a weak verb. Maybe we can change it around and use the damages as an adjective: "*A $1 million fire injured two people....*" Be careful not to use the wrong verb. It would be incorrect to use *destroyed*. The facts don't indicate the restaurant was destroyed — only damaged.

Or we may decide the fact that two people were injured is more important. And so we might say:

> *Two people were injured in a $1 million fire Tuesday...*

Don't interpret the facts and draw judgments or conclusions. It would be improper to write, *A waiter's carelessness resulted in a $1 million fire...* That's adding your own comments and conclusions to the story, what journalists call *editorializing*. It is unethical reporting. Unfortunately, if you've spent much time reading, watching, or listening to the news these days you know that too many reporters do it.

It should be noted that this is the structure of a print news lead. Broadcast leads are a bit different (we'll talk about them later), though they must still grab the viewer or listener's attention. Generally speaking, the shorter the lead is, the easier it is to understand quickly. If the reader has to go back and read a sentence twice, chances are he'll just skip the story. Remember too, in the English language, we tend to remember information better if it's placed at the beginning or end of the sentence. Information placed in the middle of the sentence often is forgotten.

• The Body •

The problem with writing the body, unlike the lead, is that the body is the rest of the story while the lead is just one paragraph. If the story is long or complex, we're dealing with a great deal of information that must be organized into some kind of structure the reader can understand.

Since we're dealing with a news story and the inverted pyramid, the idea is to provide the supporting information for the lead in descending order of importance. Consequently, we must figure out what's next most important to understand the story. Then we must determine what's next most important after that, and so on. We must write the story as if we might be stopped at any moment, and so, we must get the most important information out first.

This does not mean that a story should sound like a laundry list of facts, however. We've got to craft the story in such a way that it's easy to read, makes sense, and logically flows from one topic or subject area to the next.

To do this, writers must learn to keep related information together. For example, if we are talking about a person in the story, we must find all the information that pertains to him and lump it together. When we're talking about a particular topic, the reader wants to know all about that topic at that moment. He doesn't want to have to sift through the rest of the story, find the information piecemeal, and put it together himself to make sense of it. When I'm reading about John Jones, I want to know about John Jones.

This doesn't happen when we're taking notes, of course. During the interview all sorts of seemingly unrelated information comes out. Different things about a person emerge at different times. At one point we learn his name. Five minutes later we learn his age. A half an hour later we learn his address. In between we learn all sorts of different information. We try to keep information organized by keeping our questions organized, but any journalist will tell you that stories don't just flow logically out of dozens of pages of notes on their own. It's the writer's job to take those notes and organize them so they make sense.

The easiest way to do that is to take different colored pens and circle the information in your notes that goes together. For example, all the information about one person in the story will be circled in blue while all the information about another person will be circled red. Then go back and put all the same colored information together into some sort of coherent order.

Remember, as a writer, you are looking for the best way to organize the story so it makes sense to your reader. It has to be accurate, but it also has to be readable. You should be looking for the natural flow to the story. Don't worry about transitions or introductions. Just begin a new paragraph and start talking about the next piece of new information.

Also, it's better to write from your understanding of the story than to write from the notes. Review the notes until you fully understand what the story is about. Once you know the story well enough to tell it to yourself, write it as if you are telling someone what you've learned, checking the notes periodically to make sure you're not missing something or getting the story wrong. Once you have finished the story, go back and compare it with the notes to make sure everything is one hundred percent accurate, denotatively and connotatively. Writers who are glued to their notes produce stories that sound like, well, a list of notes. The story is stiff and difficult to read.

Having said this, DON'T INTERJECT YOUR OWN OPINION, INTERPRETATION, OR ANAYLSIS. Write facts. Use simple sentences, concrete nouns, and action verbs.

The Journalist's Primer

Remember, good writers understand the *objective correlative*. Bad writers don't. The objective correlative is writing about the object (fact) that correlatives to the meaning one is trying to convey. For example, it would be commentary and inappropriate to say the evening sky was beautiful. That is the writer's interpretation. Also, the word *beautiful* is an empty word. It means nothing. What is beautiful? To one person, the word means one thing; to another, it means something else.

Better to use facts that can't be misinterpreted: *The orange wafer sun slipped into the aquamarine sea sending up layers of red, orange, pink, yellow, violet and blue.* Now we all see the same thing; we know exactly what the writer is telling us.

Don't say the shooter was *antisocial*. You're not a psychologist who's done an in-depth study of the man. Note the facts and let the reader reach his own conclusions: The accused *lived alone, told neighbors to get off of his lawn, and only came outside on Sundays.* Write that and we'll understand. There's less room for misunderstanding when we're using facts.

As you write through the story remember that you must attribute the information — that is, tell us where you got it. Attribution generally comes last in the sentence, i.e., *The sky is falling,* Chicken Little said. Of course, if it were someone important offering the information — such as the president — you would put his name first since it is news when an important person says something.

To avoid confusion, it's important to alert the reader right away if there is a change in speaker in the story. For example, *The sky is falling,* Chicken Little said. Briar Rabbit said, *A piece hit me on the head.* If you fail to do this, the audience will still think Chicken Little is speaking even though the new information is from Briar Rabbit. They won't know there's a new speaker until they get to the end of the next sentence.

You need not attribute every sentence, but it always should be clear to the audience who is speaking or where the information is coming from. Use *said*. People are used to seeing it and hearing it. It may seem redundant to you, but everyone else reads right over it without a thought. Don't say *smiled, exclaimed, shouted*, etc. It's impossible to smile a word.

Be careful not to assume things and write yourself into a corner. For example, if someone robs a convenience store and kills the clerk, don't say police are looking for an unknown assailant. Assailant is singular. More than one person may be responsible. Say instead that police are looking for whoever shot and killed the clerk. *Whoever* can be singular or plural.

Finally, don't use slang unless it's part of a quote. Neither should you use phrases that can have double meanings. And be precise. Make sure you are saying what you think you are saying. *He was shot between 3:30 a.m. and 4:15 a.m.* is a long time to be shot — 45 minutes. Probably the writer meant to say that he was shot *sometime* or *once* between those times.

• Endings •

Typically, the inverted pyramid structure does not have a formal conclusion. When we run out of facts necessary to tell the story, we stop. Since stories are often trimmed from the bottom to fit the allotted space, providing a formal ending that may get cut anyway is often a waste of time.

Nevertheless, careful writers will often look for a quote or appropriate ending for their stories. This is not to say they will attempt to sum up the story with their own analysis. That would be adding their own comment and unethical. But looking for a way to bring the story down to a logical ending is inherent in good story telling.

The best approach is to look for ways to end the story even as you begin looking for ways to get into it. Put another way, as you are looking for your lead among the facts, look also for your conclusion. Good stories tend to end where they began, talking about the same thing. They make a nice, complete circle and tie back to the beginning. For example, if the lead notes that a restaurant fire was caused when a waiter tripped and spilled hot grease on some curtains, we might use a quote from the fire chief — *It was just a freak accident.* — as a way to end the story. By referring back to the action that caused the fire and prompted the story in the first place, we return to where we started and tie the story together.

To make the ending sound even better, we bury the attribution instead of tacking it on to the end of the quote. For example, *It was,* Fire Chief John Jackson said, *just a freak accident.*

The Journalist's Primer

People tend to remember beginnings and endings better than middles. So it's better to leave them with the uniqueness of the story — the freak accident — than the fire chief's name.

Note the following story in inverted pyramid form and how the story moves from general information in the lead to specific details in the body and the least important information at the bottom, ending with a closing quote.

> *A fire injured two people and caused $1 million in damages Tuesday at a downtown Oklahoma City restaurant after a waiter said he tripped and spilled hot grease on some curtains, firefighters said.*
>
> *John Jones, 42, of 425 Maple St., and waiter Dan Dean, 24, of 678 Pine St., were both treated at the OU Medical Center for smoke inhalation and released, hospital officials said.*
>
> *The fire started in the kitchen area of the Big Eats restaurant at 90 N.W. Hickory St. about 2 p.m., firefighters said. Dean said he tripped on a loose floorboard as he was carrying hot grease from the stove out a side exit to a waste bin in the parking area. The grease splashed on curtains next to the door and set them on fire, he said.*
>
> *"Before I could put the bucket down and pull the curtains off the wall it had spread," Dean said. "It was just so quick. It was all I could do to get out."*
>
> *Restaurant manager Tom Black said the fire spread to the rear dining area as nine diners, including Jones, and six employees retreated through the front exit.*
>
> *Firefighters received a 911 call at 2:01 p.m. and were on the scene at 2:05 p.m., fire department records show. Fire Chief John Jackson said the fire was extinguished by 2:45 p.m. Damage in the kitchen, dining area, and roof was extensive, Boyd said. Insurance investigator Joe Green said he estimated damage at $1 million.*
>
> *Black said the restaurant would open again in about three months after repairs.*
>
> *"It was," said Jackson, "just one of those freak accidents."*

• Structures for Different Stories •

Sometimes what happens at a news event will have an effect on the story's structure. For example, city council meetings usually include an agenda listing several items. Some of the items will be more important than others. Maybe the council is considering building a new park and the members spend most of the meeting discussing that one issue. Before adjourning, however, they will run through the remaining agenda. The reporter, weighing the relative news value of each of the items, may conclude that the park discussion was the big story of the evening and spend most of his efforts writing about that. But he can't simply ignore everything else that happened at the meeting. That, after all, is news, too. So after discussing the park, he simply lists what else the council did and tacks it onto the end of the story. This is called *shirt-tailing.*

At other times, the timing of the story can be important. Sometimes reporters will do an *advance* about a story that will happen in the future. Perhaps it's to alert the audience about a play or meeting so they can make arrangements to attend. In those cases, the *when* of the story is important and will receive emphasis along with any information that may be important to the reader to prepare for the meeting.

In other cases, just the opposite situation may occur. To keep readers up to date on an ongoing story, reporters will do a *follow* or *follow-up* to tell them of any new developments. Most stories don't happen all at once. They unfold over days or weeks or years. As new information becomes available or changes, the reporter is obligated to explain it.

As a result, follow-up stories focus on the latest development first in the lead while also providing just enough information to remind the reader of the original news event. For example, *The search will continue Tuesday for the body of an Oklahoma City man who is believed to have drowned Monday in Lake Arcadia after falling from a boat.* Even if the story is years old, the reporter must include enough information about the original event that prompted the story so those who may just now be reading it for the first time can understand it in context. Theoretically, you should be able to step off a space ship from Mars, having just arrived on Earth, and pick up the story and understand it (assuming you could speak human language).

The Journalist's Primer

The lack of follow-ups is a big problem in journalism today. News happens so quickly that news outlets often drop old stories in their effort to cover new ones. We learn that a person was arrested but the reporter never bothers to tell us how the case turned out. This can be frustrating for those who try to follow the news and stay informed. The general rule is that once a reporter decides to cover a story he should stay with it until it's over. This doesn't mean that he has to report on it every day, but it does mean he needs to regularly check on it and report on any new developments as they occur.

Another type of story is the *round-up*. Often referred to as multiple-element stories, they involve putting several related stories into one story. Since the stories are all about the same general topic, it saves space to lump them together and talk about them all at once. For example, *A series of tornadoes tore across Oklahoma Tuesday, killing five, injuring more than 200, and causing more than $10 million in property damage, civil defense officials said.* The story would then detail what happened with each tornado, starting with the most destructive.

Brites are short, anecdotal stories usually focusing on something humorous, strange, or ironical. Sometimes they are constructed in the inverted pyramid. But they are often constructed like a joke with the punch line of the story coming last. Then they are called "suspended-interest" stories.

For example, a brite may sound like this:

> *"A 22-year-old circus worker pleaded guilty in municipal court Thursday to breaking and entering after police said they discovered him hiding inside a magician's trunk in a clown shop.*
>
> *Billy Jones, of 432 Maple St., stared at his feet as Judge Judy Jones sentenced him to 30 days in jail.*
>
> *Police said they were alerted to the man after witnesses said they heard pounding coming from inside the shop. After locating the source of the sounds, police said they spent nearly 20 minutes trying to figure out how to open the box.*
>
> *Police said Jones told them that once he got inside the trunk he couldn't figure out how to get out. He said it was designed to make people "disappear."*

• Exercise •

List on the board the who, what, when, where, how, and why of a story, and have the students construct a lead. Review. Add more facts and write the rest of the story using the inverted pyramid.

Then, snip ten stories out of the newspaper and cut each story up, paragraph by paragraph. Put each cut up story into an envelope and number it. Pass the envelopes out to the class after you have divided the class into teams of two. Give each team a copy of the newspaper containing the stories. Have each team take out the cut up story and try to put it back together into the inverted pyramid order. Then have the students take out the newspaper, find the story they worked on, and see how closely they came to matching the structure of the story as it appeared in the paper. Have each team do all ten stories.

• Telling Stories with Words, Sounds, and Pictures •

Broadcast comes in two forms: radio and television. Radio works with words and sounds. Television, of course, works with words, sounds, and pictures. But writing for television doesn't mean you just add pictures to a radio script. The two media tell stories differently.

Radio tells stories much the same way as newspapers, and in a sense, radio has more in common with newspapers. Stories are selected for their news value regardless of whether the reporter has the necessary background sounds to add to the story. He still primarily uses words to create images in the mind's eye, much as a newspaper reporter does. In both cases the reader and the listener must translate the words to "see" the story.

But in television, pictures tell the story. Consequently, reporters select their stories first on the basis of what pictures they've got. Television then marries words to pictures — that is, the words they use must support the pictures. You can't write about one thing and show pictures of something else.

Because TV is so reliant on pictures, television writing is more limited than writing for radio and newspapers. If you don't have the pictures, you must change the way you write the story. No one wants to sit in front of a television and listen to the story. They want to see it. Without pictures, the best you can do is write a radio story for television. And that doesn't work so well.

Remember, in TV pictures lead the words.

Because we're using more than words — both in radio and TV — the structure of the story is different. In radio, you include sounds; in television, you include sounds and pictures to go along with the spoken words. Therefore, broadcast writing does not use the inverted pyramid form found in newspaper writing. Also, broadcast journalists write for the ear. The writing must be clear and concise, simple and conversational. Unlike writing for print, the listener or viewer can't go back and see the story again. He must understand it the first time.

When writing to the pictures, the reporter must remember to supplement the pictures with the words and sounds that are needed to communicate the idea. The more specific the picture, the more general the description; the more general the picture, the more specific and descriptive the writing should be. Unlike newspaper stories, broadcast stories are written with a beginning, middle, and end. They should generally be told in active voice using present or present perfect tense.

Broadcast writing comes in two basic forms: writing for newscasts, usually delivered live, and pre-produced packages. Both of these basic forms are found in radio and TV.

• Radio •

Radio writing gives us news briefs and short newscasts. It can also include longer produced stories lasting several minutes such as those found on NPR and even longer documentaries. Radio writing is short, direct, and punchy. News updates are usually less than four minutes, and each story generally runs less than 30 seconds.

The basic story form consists of short, declarative sentences that introduce and explain the story using essential facts. This may lead to a short, pithy sound bite and a brief concluding statement known as a *tag*. Generally, the shorter the news segment, the shorter the stories. These short radio stories may be no more than a series of one-sentence headlines. Stories with sound, referred to as *actualities* or *sound bites*, are longer and placed more prominently in the newscast. Produced stories using the reporter's voice and sound are typically called *wrap-arounds* in radio.

Radio newscasts also require the anchor to set up the wrap-around with what is called a *lead-in*, in effect a brief summary of the story that leads into the more detailed information found in the story.

Here is an example of a short radio wrap-around starting with an anchor lead-in:

> **Anchor:** *Wild fires have destroyed 20,000 acres of forests in southwestern Indiana. Investigators suspect arson was the cause. WXYZ's Joe Smith has learned that officials have found a gas can near the garbage dump where the fire started.*
>
> **Wrap-around:** *Gibson county fire officials scouring the area where Highland Hills fire began now have what they call a promising lead in the case. Eyewitnesses have told investigators that they saw a man pouring gasoline onto a sofa near the road where they believe the fire began. Fire Marshall Bill Dunbar says a blackened, empty gas can has been found.*
>
> **Sound-on-tape (SOT):** *"We believe this is a major break in the case. Arson is the likely cause. We have now called in the FBI to help us in the investigation."*
>
> *(0:20)*
> **Outcue:** *"...help us in the investigation."*
>
> **Wrap-around:** *It is estimated that the Highland Hills fire has caused 6.8 million dollars in damage. Insurance adjusters and state officials are expected to tour the site on Tuesday. This is Joe Smith, WXYZ News.*

Tip: When writing radio copy, the writer should not split sentences over two pages. It breaks the natural flow of the sentence if the reader has to pause to turn the page.

NPR presents the best examples of long-form radio reporting. Conversational writing, natural or *wild* sound that engages the listener, and an emphasis on explanatory journalism create the NPR style. NPR writing is distinguished by its *take you there* journalism using sounds and audio mixing.

Here is an example of a long-form radio reporting:

> *MARY JONES, host:*
>
> *Madison County has a new tool to help victims of storms — Facebook.*
> *Civil emergency managers used it to give assistance after last year's ice storm, and last week Facebook helped them warn residents of the monster tornado that destroyed much of Billings.*
> *WXYZ Radio's Angela Blackburn explains how the social media site has changed the way civil defense information is spread during and after the storm.*
>
> *(Sound of tornado sirens)*
>
> *ANGELA: Madison County residents woke up to the sound of tornado sirens last Tuesday. Those on Facebook also got a warning.*
>
> *BARRY SMITH: I was checking my Facebook news feed early on Tuesday when I saw the heads-up to take shelter.*
>
> *ANGELA: Only two people were injured as the tornado tore through Billings.*
>
> *(Sound of tornado)*
>
> *ANGELA: Emergency managers credit Facebook with getting people into shelters. And it also played a critical role after the storm moved through.*

EMERGENCY MANAGER HERMAN DUNN: You could not get a cell phone call in or out of Billings. You could only get text messages. But we could use Facebook to pass information from Billings back here to search crews that were preparing to deploy via chat on Facebook. That was our only method of communication.

ANGELA: Emergency management director Ron Kosinski wasn't sold on Facebook a year ago.

RON KOSINSKI: I was not really a social networking guy, but that may be because of my age. I always thought Facebook was for kids.

ANGELA: Kosinski's assistant convinced him to give Facebook a try.

RON KOSINSKI: She told me a lot of people get their information from Facebook — it's not just for students. She thought we could reach a lot more people, and she was right.

ANGELA: Kosinski's assistant Heather Johnson says Facebook worked even better than she expected.

HEATHER JOHNSON: We've got over 1,700 fans. We may be up to almost 1,800 now that the word is getting out.

ANGELA: Tuesday evening those fans were watching radar and seeing pictures of the rotating clouds circling the city.

HEATHER JOHNSON: Our fans were out there saying "ya gotta see this" and posting pictures of scary-looking clouds. They were also warning people who were at the high school graduation that they needed to take cover.

ANGELA: Once the storm had passed, emergency managers posted safety information on Facebook and let residents know where to find supplies and shelter.

RON KOSINSKI: It really made a difference. Facebook cut down the response time to help survivors. We also saw a big increase in

> *the number of people who came to our civil defense shelter to get food, water, and blankets.*
>
> *ANGELA: Kosinski expects Facebook to become an even bigger part of the county's civil defense planning. He thinks as more people get smart phones with Facebook apps, emergency information will be just a touch-screen away. For WXYZ Radio News, I'm Angela Blackburn.*

• Television •

Adding pictures makes television news writing much more complicated than writing for radio. Plus, television newscasts require different kinds of writing. In order, we will address the creation of video stories, scripting, live shots, and teases.

Television writing gives us on-camera **readers** — stories read without pictures; **voice-overs** (VO) — stories that have accompanying video; **voice-over sound-on-tape** (VOSOT) — a voice-over that has sound on tape; **packages** — pre-produced video stories; and **live shots** — live reports from a remote location.

Reader – The reader is the most basic form of broadcast news writing. It is a story read by the news anchor without video or sound bites, intended to provide information in brief. A reader is not a traditional story with a beginning, middle, and end. The form is: declarative statement, explanatory information, and conclusion. Readers are similar to radio news briefs. They are also often used as *pacers* which vary length within a newscast and help keep it moving.

> Example: *Governor Jones has announced she is running for re-election. Jones wants a second term to continue her work on reducing taxes and developing pro-growth, pro-business policies. The 52-year-old Republican is seeking a second term. Four years ago, she became the state's first female governor.*

If the story is more than a reader, that is, it involves video, the reporter needs to prepare what is called a *shot sheet* after acquiring the video. The shot sheet shows a short description of the pictures, the length of each shot, and where to find it on the media time code — a time noted on the video. Here is an example:

27:54:32 - 27:54:46	Dog barking (:14)
27:54:46 - 28:55:02	House on fire (:16)
28:55:02 - 28:55:12	Fireman hosing ashes (:10)
28:55:12 - 28:55:20	"I don't know where to go. I've lost it all." (:08)
28:55:20 - 28:55:32	"I'm just glad that my family was able to get out safely. We hope that insurance will cover the loss, but we won't know until we talk to the adjuster." (:12)
28:55:32 - 28:55:38	Flashing lights on fire truck (:06)

A shot sheet may be brief or could go several pages. It provides the blueprint for the reporter and photographer/editor to use in writing the story and editing the pictures to match the words.

Voice-over – Voice-overs are the simplest video stories, but not necessarily the easiest to write. They are stories with supporting, explanatory video, either new, unedited video or video from archives.

Armed with video to tell the story, referenced on the shot sheet, the reporter must *write to the video*. That means writing words in a logical sequence to tell the story, while referencing video you see that supports the words.

Video stories require a two-column format, with words on the right side of the page and video instructions on the left. Writing to video requires each sentence or thought to be accompanied by video that explains, reinforces, or complements the words. If you don't have the right video, make it a reader.

Example of a VO: [UL](STEVE)
(TAKE VO 0:18)   (VO)

(0:00-0:08 XYZ Airlines Planes)   THE ONGOING LABOR DISPUTE
                                    BETWEEN XYZ AIRLINES AND ITS
                                    MECHANICS HAS MOVED INTO A
                                    NEW CHAPTER.
                                    BUT IT'S NO FAIRY TALE ENDING.
(0:08-0:13 Union Leaders)   UNION LEADERS ADMIT THE
                                    VOTE OF ITS MEMBERS WILL
                                    LIKELY SAVE THE AIRLINE BUT
                                    WILL NOT PREVENT LAYOFFS.
(0:13-0:18 Striking mechanics   MECHANICS REJECTED A
with pickets)   TENTATIVE CONTRACT IN
                                    DECEMBER AND THE AIRLINE
                                    COUNTERED WITH A NEW
                                    PROPOSAL LAST MONTH.

Voice-overs can be done for video or graphics. Graphics commonly show maps, photos, quotes, charts, and numbers. They are especially helpful for stories with numbers and percentages. Viewers don't like to do math. Numbers are difficult to remember. So, using a clear, explanatory graphic can be powerful. Just be sure the words match the graphic. Graphics can confuse viewers when the written copy paraphrases the message seen on the graphic. If the copy says "the cost of living rose 3% in July," the graphic should show it just that way. Likewise, if the graphic shows a quote, the quote should be written verbatim in the copy. Make sure graphics are not too busy, and only reference one fact or thought at a time.

Voice-over with sound on tape – A voice-over with a sound bite or "sound on tape" is commonly called a VOSOT, or a VO-Bite. In a VOSOT, the voice-over copy leads up to and introduces the sound bite. The goal should be to write a declarative sentence that stands on its own preceding the sound bite. (In radio, it is important to make the preceding statement make sense by itself, in case the sound bite does not play properly on-air.) This style is preferred for VOSOT's, too. The sound bite should *prove* the lead-in line by elaborating on it or reinforcing the statement. VOSOT's need strong quotes. If the person being quoted does not make a strong statement, it is better not to write the story as a VOSOT, but to paraphrase their statement and write the story as a VO or reader. VOSOT's need a VO or on-camera tag to complete the story.

Example of a VOSOT:

| | (STEVE) |
| (TAKE VO 0:18) | (VO) |

(0:00-0:08 XYZ Airlines Planes)	THE ONGOING LABOR DISPUTE BETWEEN XYZ AIRLINES AND ITS MECHANICS HAS MOVED INTO A NEW CHAPTER. BUT IT'S NO FAIRY TALE ENDING.
(0:08-0:13 Union Leaders)	UNION LEADERS ADMIT THE VOTE OF ITS MEMBERS WILL LIKELY SAVE THE AIRLINE BUT WILL NOT PREVENT LAYOFFS.
(0:13-0:18 Striking mechanics with pickets)	MECHANICS REJECTED A TENTATIVE CONTRACT IN DECEMBER AND THE AIRLINE COUNTERED WITH A NEW PROPOSAL LAST MONTH.
(0:18-0:26 Dan Duncan)	MECHANICS UNION PRESIDENT DAN DUNCAN SAYS WITHOUT CONCESSIONS FROM THE AIRLINE, THE STRIKE WILL CONTINUE.
(0:26-0:36 Duncan sound bite)	(SOT 0:26-0:36) "Our union wants to keep its jobs and we are willing to meet the front office halfway to keep the airline solvent, but we are not willing to vote on a new contract until we have a chance to evaluate the latest proposal."
(VO 0:36-0:42 Picket lines)	(STEVE VO) UNION MEMBERS SAY THEY ARE WILLING TO TAKE A THREE PERCENT PAY CUT, BUT WILL NOT AGREE TO A REDUCTION IN RETIREMENT BENEFITS.

Package – The most highly-produced video stories are called "packages." Packages are where broadcast reporters make their living. They combine video, audio, natural sound, graphics, and music to create narrative stories.

Packages require reporters and photographers to collaborate in video storytelling. Reporters and photographers should communicate before, during, and after shooting video and interviews in the field to make sure they are on the same page creatively. Again, reporters need to match their words with the video.

If a writer does not have the proper video to complement, illustrate, or reinforce his words, he will need to change the copy. Yes, that limits the kinds of stories that can be told, and how a package is put together, but packages require the right combination of words, pictures, and sounds. Good writers will either get the needed video or drop the idea of doing a package altogether. Reporters who cannot turn out strong packages on deadline do not last long in broadcasting.

Television reporters should begin thinking about crafting the story while they are still in the field or returning from it. If a reporter has an idea on how to write the story, he should get started as quickly as possible in laying out the structure, along with key words and phrases. It helps if the writer formulates the central idea of the story and composes a short sentence explaining what the story is about.

Once at the station, reporters should make a video log of the shots and an audio log of the interviews and other sound with time code to assist the editor. If there is time, transcribing interviews verbatim is helpful (and required on scripts where sound bites are included). Then it's time to organize the pictures and sound and start writing. If the story doesn't come together, tell it to someone first, then get started. Another technique would be to review your video and let the pictures tell the story back to you.

Writers should use a 2-column or split-page script for packages just as they do for a VO or VOSOT with the text on the right side and technical instructions on the left side.

Packages are about storytelling with a beginning, middle, and end. The story should be written naturally, as if you're telling a story in your own words.

The top of the story should grab the attention of the viewer. Usually, it begins with the strongest video or natural sound. Good reporters should always be thinking about how they are going to begin and end their stories. A rule of thumb is best video first, second-best video last.

The lead sentence establishes what the story is about and gives viewers a hint of where the story is heading. The body of the package should relate back to the lead, blending facts, pictures, and sound that support the premise of the story and relate the story to the viewer. The best stories reveal certain information at the right time, withhold certain information until the right time, create suspense or conflict, engage viewers by showing how the conflict affects people, and provide a resolution.

Writing to video is difficult, but essential, in video storytelling. Writers can use the *touch and go* technique to help match the pictures to the words. Touch and go requires the writer to write a line that is supported by properly referenced video. After referencing the video specifically, the writer can elaborate more generally without needing to match each shot perfectly.

Example of the Touch and Go technique:

	(STEVE)
(TAKE VO 0:18)	(VO)
(0:00-0:08 XYZ Airlines Planes)	THE ONGOING LABOR DISPUTE BETWEEN XYZ AIRLINES AND ITS MECHANICS HAS MOVED INTO A NEW CHAPTER.
	BUT IT'S NO FAIRY TALE ENDING.
(0:08-0:13 Union Leaders)	UNION LEADERS ADMIT THE VOTE OF ITS MEMBERS WILL LIKELY SAVE THE AIRLINE BUT WILL NOT PREVENT LAYOFFS.
(0:13-0:18 Striking mechanics with pickets)	MECHANICS REJECTED A TENTATIVE CONTRACT IN DECEMBER AND THE AIRLINE COUNTERED WITH A NEW PROPOSAL LAST MONTH.

(0:18-0:26 Dan Duncan)	MECHANICS UNION PRESIDENT DAN DUNCAN SAYS WITHOUT CONCESSIONS FROM THE AIRLINE, THE STRIKE WILL CONTINUE.
(0:26-0:36 Duncan sound bite)	(SOT 0:26-0:36) "Our union wants to keep its jobs and we are willing to meet the front office halfway to keep the airline solvent, but we are not willing to vote on a new contract until we have a chance to evaluate the latest proposal."
(VO 0:36-0:42 Picket lines)	(STEVE VO) UNION MEMBERS SAY THEY ARE WILLING TO TAKE A THREE PERCENT PAY CUT, BUT WILL NOT AGREE TO A REDUCTION IN RETIREMENT BENEFITS.

In the above example, the phrases "union leaders," "mechanics" and "union members" are referenced with video. Once that video has been mentioned (*touched*) in the script, the writer can *go* on to tell what they (union leaders, mechanics, and union members) are doing or saying without specifically showing it.

For example, if the sentence says *Pigs are flying*, it will require pictures of pigs flying to support the words. If the sentence says, *Dan Duncan says pigs are flying*, we only need to see a picture of Dan Duncan.

Natural sound makes packages come alive. Look for opportunities to record natural sound in the field and use it in writing stories. Imagine what our world would be like without sounds going on around us. Natural sound gives packages context and texture, and engages viewers.

Standups are another integral part of packages. Never open a package with a standup; avoid closing standups whenever possible. Remember, the beginning and ending of a package should be the strongest visually. Standups are not very interesting. Bob Dotson of *NBC News* has long stressed that "the reporter is not the story."

Effective standups are used to express a thought that cannot easily be illustrated with video or to transition from one thought or location to another. Be sure to do standups in a location that supports the thought expressed, and reference your location, if you can do it naturally, to let the viewer know where you are and why you are there. Also, make sure that the sound is good, framing is flattering, and the background is free of distractions. Write to the standup so that your copy flows naturally into it. If the standup is gratuitous, forced, or just doesn't feel right — kill it! Remember: The reporter is NOT the story.

The story should end with strong video, generally a neutral or negative-action shot (moving away from the viewer) that provides a fulfilling resolution. The end may involve symmetry, by bringing the first video or thought expressed in the package forward to the end, to form a concluding statement that ties up the central idea of the story in a satisfying way. The end should not only use strong video, but should include meaningful natural sound, an impactful spoken quote, or a concluding statement by the reporter that creates a logical ending. Generally, it is best not to end with a sound bite.

> Example of an effective ending: *After several attempts to reach the lawyers for the company, we were told to submit questions in writing. Company officials said they would respond in two weeks. The trial in the lawsuit will begin on January 15.*

When you have completed writing your story, read it out loud. Does it sound like something you would say to someone? Does it make sense? Would a viewer understand it, with no opportunity for a second chance to see or hear it? Edit to eliminate unnecessary words and ensure clarity.

When writing a package you also should hold something back for a tag or wrap-up — the line or two following the package that provides additional information. A link to a website, updated information, a concluding statement that is not supported by video, a reaction to the story — consider these for the tag.

> Example of a tag: *Legislators will begin an interim study on the water issue by the end of the year.*

Reporters should also hold something back to use in the lead-in, also called an *intro*. The lead-in sets up what the story is about. A lead-in typically incorporates information or sound bites that was not used in the package. This information should provide meaning and context to the package. Lead-ins are more than just throwaway lines with a *so and so reports* attached. *In other news…* and *standing by live…* don't tell us anything. Reporters should also avoid sensational attention-grabbers: *Breaking news tonight…a tragic murder.* Aren't all murders tragic? The lead-in should transition logically from the previous story in the newscast to your package, and flow seamlessly into your story.

An example of a good lead-in:

> *About two million Americans will have no place to sleep tonight. Many of them are children and people with mental illness, including veterans. Homelessness strikes every community. But it's especially acute in big cities. WXYZ's Suzanne Walker has found that a new program is showing promise in fixing the problem.*

Example of a package with split-page editing instructions:

Number for the video clip to be used

Time code of video used

TC 11:14:27 Nats of Gibson children splashing in the lake (0:04)

<c0013 11:14:27
Nats of splashing (:04)>

Description of video

Length of video

TC 13:42:28 Gibson boat leaves dock (0:08)

This is what the REPORTER says

GREG AND BECKY GIBSON ENJOY FAMILY OUTINGS WITH THEIR CHILDREN AT FITTS LAKE. SWIMMING AND BOATING — SOMETIMES THEY EVEN GET IN A LITTLE FISHING.

Length of sound bite

Person speaking

TC 11:04:22 Billy Gibson with fish (0:03)

<c0003 11:04:22 (:03)
Billy: "Wow, look at that one!">

What person says in sound bite

TC 11:04:32 Becky takes fish from Billy, gives it to Greg (0:05)

GREG AND BECKY ARE AWARE OF HOW QUICKLY FUN CAN TURN TO TRAGEDY.

<c0004 11:05:37 (:17)
Becky: "There have been a lot of drownings here, and its just terrible, you know, to think of even one child drowning. I know friends of mine have had children drown so we're looking at life vests because it only takes a freaky little second to lose a life.">

TC 11:14:36 Lee Ryan getting into boat (0:09)	LEE RYAN IS A PARK RANGER AT FITTS LAKE. HE SAYS A CHILD CAN DROWN IN AS LITTLE AS 20 SECONDS, EVEN IN VERY SHALLOW WATER. <c0002 11:00:09 (:06) Ryan: "Kids can drown in an inch of water, so even when you're swimming at the beach you need to have that life jacket on.">
TC 11:16:33 Greg Gibson steering boat (0:04)	GREG GIBSON ALWAYS WEARS A LIFE VEST WHEN HE'S ON THE LAKE.
TC 11:16:44 Cindy in boat (0:02)	<c0005 11:08:12 (:07) Greg Gibson: "I feel more comfortable doing it. Kinda like wearing a seat belt in your car, it just kinda gives you security.">
TC 11:12:29 Cindy and Billy in boat, wearing vests (0:03)	WEARING VESTS EARNED THE GIBSON KIDS A TREAT.
TC 11:01:08 Tight shot of Gibson children getting coupon and smiling at Ryan as he talks (0:03)	<c0002 11:00:40 (:15) Ryan: "We have a little program going on called, 'You have been ticketed for wearing a life jacket.' and what this is is since all of you are under 13, you all are going to get a free frosty from Wendy's. Kids: Thank you.

	Ryan: "Thank YOU for being smart and safe!">
TC 11:18:39 Skiers skimming across lake (0:06)	THIS IS ONE OF TWO MAJOR WATER SAFETY CAMPAIGNS THE LAKE PATROL IS ROLLING OUT THIS HOLIDAY WEEKEND.
TC 11:18:09 Adults getting into speed boat (0:06) TC 11:08:56 Tight shot of boater drinking beer (0:03)	<c0001 10:53:22 (:12) Ryan: "Last year we had a total of 15 drownings and this year we've already exceeded that number and we're not even done with the recreational season, so what we're trying to do is just promote water safety.">
TC 11:09:34 Boaters standing in boat, putting on life vests (0:10)	RYAN SAYS ADULTS ARE MORE LIKELY TO DROWN THAN CHILDREN, BECAUSE THEY ARE LESS LIKELY TO WEAR LIFE VESTS. DRINKING IS ALSO A PROBLEM, ESPECIALLY FOR YOUNG MEN.
	<c0014 11:17:14 (:10) Ryan: "People who wear life vests don't drown. Which one is in your future... A life jacket or a toe tag? The choice is yours.">
TC 11:10:21 Ryan pulls his boat up to speed boat at dock, talks to boaters (0:08)	THE LAKE PATROL WILL BE OUT THIS WEEKEND, HANDING OUT TICKETS AND FINES TO BOATERS

	WHO DON'T WEAR LIFE VESTS, OR HAVE THEM EASILY ACCCESSIBLE IN THEIR BOATS.
TC 11:10:58 Tight shot sequence of boaters snapping on life vests (0:06), with shot of vests out on seats of boat (0:04)	<c0001 10:54:50 (:10) Ryan: "Every boater should wear a life vest. Even if you are not wearing one, they shouldn't be stored, they should be out and handy, so you can grab it if you need it.">
TC 11:15:49 Campers eating and drinking on beach (0:02), dog splashing in water on shore (0:03)	RYAN SAYS A WEEKEND AT THE LAKE SHOULD BE MEMORABLE FOR FUN, NOT TRAGEDY.
TC 11:16:36 Skier cutting across wake (wearing life vest) (0:06)	HE SAYS THERE'S NO EXCUSE FOR NOT HAVING A PROPER LIFE VEST.
TC 11:18:16 Skier silhouetted against setting sun, NATS up at end (0:04)	THE LAKE PATROL ALSO OFFERS FREE LOANERS SO EVERYONE CAN ENJOY THE LAKE, AND STAY SAFE ON THE WATER.

AT FITTS LAKE, RANDY JONES, WXYZ NEWS. |

Script format – Once the reporter has reviewed the shot sheet and selected the video and audio he wants to use to tell his story, and written the story in the two-column format (noted above), he passes it to the editor. The editor then drops in the video and audio to match the reporter's scripted instructions. In the meantime, the reporter writes his lead-in to the package for the anchor to read in the newscast.

Again, be sure to put your script in the proper split-page form with text that the anchor reads on the right side and director's instructions on the left. The left side has the *slug* to help identify the story in the newscast, along with tape time, video instructions, words super-imposed over pictures (*supers*), and any coding that may be necessary for the director to locate the story on the computer that stores the story for playback.

The left side also includes supers, that is, words that identify locations, speakers, and give proper credit for video acquired from other sources. Times should accompany these supers to let the director know when to show them. In addition, the finished script will show the name of the anchor that reads the story, verbatim summaries for sound bites, accurate length, and last words for the package.

Double-check copy to make sure that words are spelled correctly. Punctuate properly. Anchors "read" punctuation through the inflection in their voice. Misspelled words or improper punctuation can prevent them from reading in a smooth, conversational way. Just one misplaced, poorly punctuated, or misspelled word can ruin a story and package that is otherwise perfect.

Example of a package in newscast format (split page with technical instructions):

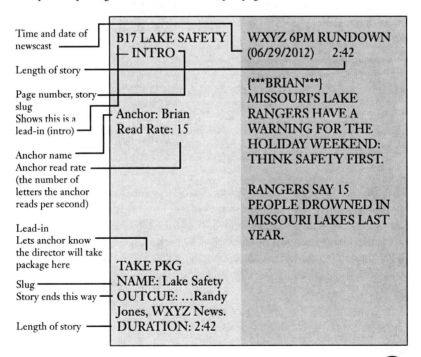

| | B17 LAKE SAFETY | WXYZ 6PM RUNDOWN |
| | INTRO | (06/29/2012)   2:42 |

Time and date of newscast

Length of story

Page number, story slug

Shows this is a lead-in (intro)

Anchor name

Anchor read rate (the number of letters the anchor reads per second)

Lead-in Lets anchor know the director will take package here

Slug

Story ends this way

Length of story

Anchor: Brian
Read Rate: 15

{***BRIAN***}
MISSOURI'S LAKE RANGERS HAVE A WARNING FOR THE HOLIDAY WEEKEND: THINK SAFETY FIRST.

RANGERS SAY 15 PEOPLE DROWNED IN MISSOURI LAKES LAST YEAR.

TAKE PKG
NAME: Lake Safety
OUTCUE: ...Randy Jones, WXYZ News.
DURATION: 2:42

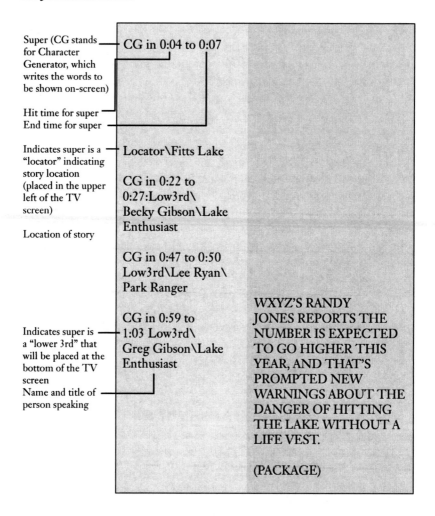

Super (CG stands for Character Generator, which writes the words to be shown on-screen)

Hit time for super
End time for super

Indicates super is a "locator" indicating story location (placed in the upper left of the TV screen)

Location of story

Indicates super is a "lower 3rd" that will be placed at the bottom of the TV screen
Name and title of person speaking

CG in 0:04 to 0:07

Locator\Fitts Lake

CG in 0:22 to 0:27:Low3rd\ Becky Gibson\Lake Enthusiast

CG in 0:47 to 0:50 Low3rd\Lee Ryan\ Park Ranger

CG in 0:59 to 1:03 Low3rd\ Greg Gibson\Lake Enthusiast

WXYZ'S RANDY JONES REPORTS THE NUMBER IS EXPECTED TO GO HIGHER THIS YEAR, AND THAT'S PROMPTED NEW WARNINGS ABOUT THE DANGER OF HITTING THE LAKE WITHOUT A LIFE VEST.

(PACKAGE)

Live Shots – Live shots are common in modern television journalism. A live shot is when a reporter talks to the anchor from the location of the story. The live shot can be with or without video. If using video, the reporter provides a brief introduction that sets up the VO, SOT, or package and gives a verbal cue to the director to show the video. After the video, the reporter concludes the story with some closing comments and tosses back to the anchor.

Reporters doing live shots may be able to memorize what they want to say, but most often they should rely on a series of brief notes to prompt what they say. Do not write out your script and read it, especially on-camera. Describe the scene. Tell what you know. Do not speculate.

Teases – Headlines and teases are used to keep viewers engaged. A headline tells the story in a few seconds, such as *The governor announces a burn-ban for twenty-two counties in western Oklahoma.* A tease entices viewers to stay tuned to learn more. Don't give away the story in the tease and don't over sell it. Viewers don't like to be confused or misled.

In teases, it is best to make viewers think they have a personal stake in the upcoming story by suggesting the viewer will learn something they need to know, such as *We'll show you how to make sure your car's tires are safe*, or *We'll take you to the big game.*

Also, don't water down your tease with conditional words such as may, can, might, possibly, could, or apparently. *Mosquitoes may possibly infect you with the West Nile virus.* Not a good tease.

Don't editorialize or make judgments. *Coming up: We'll tell you why the senator is wrong.*

Finally, although television is usually a collaborative effort involving many people, increasingly, reporters must not only report, but also shoot and edit video and even anchor.

• Storytelling Tips •

Effective writers use a variety of storytelling techniques. Some are especially important in broadcast writing. They include:

- Write for ear and keep it conversational.
- Write in short declarative sentences with one or two facts in each sentence. Cut sentences in two, if necessary.
- Use prepositions, pronouns, and contractions to make copy sound conversational, but don't overuse them.

- Keep writing simple, clear, and short. For example, see the difference between a *newspaper lead* and a *broadcast lead*:
  Newspaper: John Smith, president of Northern Moldavia, said in a meeting of high-ranking foreign ministers meeting in Brussels, that the country's economy has raised $13 billion, but spent more than $16 billion last year.
  Broadcast: *John Smith is president of Northern Moldavia. He told foreign ministers the nation is more than three billion dollars in debt.*
- Avoid clichés and hyperbole. Example: In the wake of the disaster, people in the beleaguered community heaved a sigh of relief upon learning the solitary shooter's drug-induced, ill-fated rampage had come to a screeching halt in a hail of bullets.
- Use present tense verbs when possible to show immediacy. (*Mary believes.*) Use present perfect tense to show action that is continuing without giving a time. (*Mary is telling reporters.*) Use past tense to show the action has ended. (*Mary told reporters Tuesday.*)
- Use an audio recorder to record interviews for sound bites.
- Paraphrase sound bites that are too long or awkward.
- Limit use of adjectives, adverbs, and *loaded* words and phrases that can show editorial bias. For example: *We have a sad story tonight.* Or, instead of saying someone is *unkempt* (a value judgment), tell what the person wore. Better yet, since it is TV, show them. *Joe won't spend a day in prison* suggests that the writer is disappointed or disgusted. A better, non-judgmental way to say it is *Joe will not go to prison.*
- Edit out unnecessary words. Remember, you have pictures.
- Avoid meaningless phrases such as *as expected* or *without a doubt.*
- Accurately translate technical language in easy-to-understand words. Don't use broadcast news-speak, either. Phrases like *in other news, standing by live,* or *thundershower activity* are all examples. *Thundershower activity* really means *rain.*
- Be careful with slang and humor.
- Avoid generalized statements, such as *some people say.*
- Use exact numbers when clarity is essential. Otherwise, refer to numbers generally. For example: Write *about 25-hundred,* rather than *two-thousand, five-hundred, twenty-three* or *2,523.*
- Use attribution to let the viewer know where the information came from. In broadcast writing, provide attribution in the first sentence, then use the name. For example: *The chief of police identified the shooter. Chief John Smith said...*

- Write out words — do not use abbreviations — so anchors can see the words they need to read.
- Do not hyphenate words. That makes them hard to read off the teleprompter. It can be confusing if words are hyphenated and *wrapped* onto the next line. Acronyms, however, are more easily read with hyphens between the letters (F-B-I) unless the abbreviation or acronym is so common that it needs to be written with no punctuation (OPEC).
- Use correct punctuation. Anchors use the punctuation to guide their inflection in reading to be understood.
- Use titles first when identifying people in copy. For example, in print writing: *John Smith, director of the Department of Human Services, said...* But, in broadcast writing: *DHS Director John Smith said...*
- Build sentences to emphasize the action at the end of the sentence.
- Look for opportunities to record natural sound in the field and use it in writing stories. Natural sound gives packages context and texture, and engages viewers. It also breaks up sound bites and the reporter's narration.
- Use conversational speech, but do not use slang, incorrect grammar, or off-color expressions. Your audience includes people of all ages and backgrounds.
- Spell out hard-to-pronounce words phonetically and place it in parenthesis. This helps the reader to pronounce difficult words. For example: (NEW ' – KLEE – UR) for the word *nuclear*.
- If you must write a direct quote to be read on-air, precede it with the word *quote*. For example, John Jones called the mayor, quote, *a jerk*.

Finally, remember that the ethical standards that apply to print are equally important for broadcast. A raised eyebrow here, an inflection there, or a comment anywhere interjects your own opinion into the newscast and undermines the trust of the listener and viewer in your report. Don't add to the problem of declining media credibility. Keep your report complete, factual, and objective.

• Exercise •

View a television newscast and identify each of the different story forms mentioned. Discuss any ethical problems.

Finally, have students imagine a news story with accompanying sounds and video and script and format a package.

Writing the News for the Web

• Converging Media •

The wonder of the web is that it can combine all of the advantages of traditional legacy media into one package. Newspapers can offer long, detailed reports in context that can be read, contemplated, and reviewed again, and broadcast outlets can offer audio and video with the advantage of portability and immediacy. But the web can do it all and give its audience the ability to talk back as well. In addition, web stories are not constrained by time or space, as are traditional media. You can get all the news you can stand. As a result, it's no mystery why more people are going online for their news.

Still, the advent of the web brings with it new challenges for the news industry, which is still looking for a way to make online delivery more profitable, and for journalists, who must now converge text, graphics, still photos, audio, and video into one news package while still paying attention to the basics of good reporting. They must write their stories quickly and efficiently, constantly revising and updating 24 hours a day, seven days a week. And no longer will one story do. Chances are if they're writing for the web, they must also write companion pieces for the newspaper or broadcast outlet that pays them their salary. Gone are the days of newspaper journalists and broadcast journalists. Now they're just journalists who must be able to do it all.

It also brings challenges for the reader and the democracy, particularly when it comes to trying to understand the day's news in context. The advantage of newspapers is that readers are able to understand the relative importance of each news story by its length, the boldness of its headline, and its position in the newspaper. The reader can literally spread the paper out in front of him and get an overview of one day's history. Even broadcasters can give us an indication of relative news value by which stories they place first in the broadcast. But a computer screen is too small to afford editors the ability to layout the news as they would in a newspaper. As a result, readers often get a list of stories and a hodge-podge of pictures thrown at them with no way to understand which ones are most important. Context is lost. Journalists call this *circus makeup*, and at the moment it's a big problem for web designers who may be concerned with helping people understand the news.

Fragmentation is another problem. In traditional legacy media, readers, viewers, and listeners all get the same story, which is important in a democracy. Citizens must all understand the issues of the day if they are to reach a consensus on how to handle them. But in the world of multiple media, and especially the web, not everyone has to see the same stories. They can skip the national news altogether and go straight to sports or entertainment or gardening or some other topic. Of course, just because a story was in the newspaper didn't mean that citizens would read it, but at least they would see the headline on the page. With the web, they can ignore it altogether. As a result, it becomes more difficult for them to understand the problems facing the country and reach an agreement on what to do about them.

The journalist's ability now to constantly update and revise is both good and bad. It's good because news can be delivered literally as it happens. But it's also bad because it means less time is often taken to check the accuracy of the stories or to report them in depth.

In fact, as the speed of news delivery has increased over the years, accuracy has suffered. Newspapers are generally more accurate because they come out once a day, allowing editors time to check sources and facts. Mistakes are minimal. TV and radio report stories more quickly and often several times a day, giving editors less time to check things, which adds to the number of mistakes. The web, with its ability to stream the news constantly sometimes without the use of an editor, provides an even greater challenge for maintaining accuracy. The temptation is to get the news out faster still, sacrificing even more accuracy. Pictures, as well as words, are suspect. Images can be manipulated easily on the web.

A two-tiered system has developed for online reporting. The first tier is more prone to errors. It includes information from social media outlets such as Facebook and Twitter and is immediate. The second tier is slower and allows for development of sources and information, fact-checking and editing, including revisions. It resembles the more traditional approach to journalism.

Another problem is length. Ironically, even though space is no longer a problem, online stories tend to be shorter, offering the reader less information and context. And even if all the information is there, the way online stories are written now makes it more probable that readers will get their news in small bites from multiple related sidebars. No longer will they get the complete meal from one story. This nibbling at the news means they may not stay for the full course.

These are problems that still must be overcome if the web is to fulfill our need for news in a democratic society in the twenty-first century. In the meantime, journalists must understand that web convergence has forever altered the way we receive the news.

It should be noted that we are not talking about citizen journalism or blogs here, both of which often involve commentary, though they could certainly take advantage of the online story structure discussed in this chapter. We are still talking about solid, factual reporting. So the only thing that is changing is the manner in which we report the news, not the news itself.

• Online Structure •

Despite the radical changes brought about by the Internet, not everything has changed when it comes to how we tell stories online. For one thing, we can still use the inverted pyramid, and the news comes first in the lead. In fact, getting the important news up front is even more important since search engines use key words to direct readers to the story. Too, because online page design often consists of nothing more than a list of stories, the reader may only see the first line of the story or something resembling a long headline when he first clicks on the news site. Therefore, that first line must give the gist of the story quickly so the reader has a good idea of what the story is about before he goes to it.

But the similarity often stops there. Traditional newspaper inverted pyramid stories generally provide the reader with all the news associated with an event in one story. Web stories are written in blocks of information so readers can skip around from subtopic to subtopic and sometimes from story to story, photograph to graphic, audio to video, etc.

People don't read start to finish every word you write. They don't think or read in a straight line. They may read the part at the bottom and then come back and read a part in the middle or click on a photo. The idea, therefore, is to write in clumps of information that deal with different aspects of the story in different layers. The writer may cover one aspect of the story in one section and another part in another section. Thus, online writing gives the reader more control over the story, letting him decide what to read and in what order to read it.

This is not to say that all structure and logic is lost. It's just that after the lead is written, the rest of the story need not be organized from start to finish as one big story, but rather as a logical flow of the various parts of the story. Think of it in terms of the way an editor lays out a traditional newspaper page. The page has an entry point, the lead story or a photo related to it, and then he organizes the rest of the page to direct the eye from one part or story to the next. The reader can move from one area to another at his own discretion. In this case, the reader is moving not through a page, but through a story.

• Hyperlinks •

But how does the reader move through various layers of a story on a small computer screen? Perhaps the biggest change in news story structure since the advent of the broadcast script — at least when it comes to the web —

is the development of *the hyperlink*. The link connects readers to different information, whether it's from photos, video, audio, text, or other online sources. If the first layer of the story is the gist or lead, readers can get to the other parts by moving their cursor and clicking on something else related to it. Links can be both internal, providing more information about something in the story, or external, directing the reader to more information from other outside sources.

As the reader is moving through the text itself, he can learn about related or additional information by simply clicking on links imbedded in a sentence in the story. This can help the reader put the story in context as he's reading it. Think of it as seeing a series of parenthetical insertions in the sentences as you read through the story, placed there to help you understand what you're reading by giving you more information. Hyperlinks can help you streamline your writing since there is no need online to include long explanations or definitions of where something is located or what something means. The reporter can direct the reader to that information by clicking on the hyperlink. For example: *Police said the murder scene was at Fourth and Vine*. By clicking on the hyperlink, the reader immediately sees a map of the crime scene. The trick is to not overdue it. Direct readers to only those things that need amplification or explanation.

As wonderful as this sounds, it can present a problem for journalists. For example, is the reporter responsible for the accuracy of every external link to which he refers in his story? Just how far does the reporter's responsibility for accurate reporting go? These are difficult ethical questions that journalists must still resolve. For now, the best advice is to make sure the link's source is as objective and credible as possible. For this reason, it's best to link to government or academic sites. Obviously, it makes a difference in a gun control article if one is getting information from the National Rifle Association or a group advocating gun control. Better to go with someone who doesn't have a dog in the fight and is merely there to provide information. Still, because of these and other changes journalists today must be more skeptical than ever about sources.

Moving through several links in a story is called *threading*. Liken it to the newspaper main bar and related sidebars. If the main story is about the plane crash itself, the sidebars may be related subtopics. The only difference with the web is that we get to it not by turning the page, but by clicking on a different link. Therefore, it is important to offer readers an index or guide to the different parts of the story in the main story.

Remember, too, online readers don't study stories, they scan them by *surfing the web*, picking up pieces of information as they go. The more you give them and the more they read, the better chance they have of putting the story in context. The downside, again, is that by breaking the story into manageable parts you may lessen the reader's chance of getting the whole story because you've made it easier for him to skip some of the information.

• The Quest for Context •

Regardless of what medium the journalist uses to deliver the news, good writing is still paramount. That means using short sentences and paragraphs, simple words, and keeping the subject and verb close together. We live in a fast-paced world. People want the news quickly and easily. But they also want accuracy and objectivity, so the choice and placement of words in a sentence is important. Although brevity is important, context is still most important. Don't try to cram everything onto one page of the screen. It is okay to make the reader scroll down.

Writing online also means journalists must think in terms of the total news package. They must write verbally and visually. They must think in terms of the pictures that accompany the story, the cutlines, the charts and graphs, the subheads and bullet points. They have to think in terms of how it all looks on the page and how the reader will navigate from one part to the next. Every element on the page must complement every other element. It all must work together. If the story lends itself to lists and charts, make use of them. Bulleted information is easy to grasp. Sidebars are still useful as well. Think in terms of the different topics or segments in a story and then think of a way to organize them so the reader can move from one to the other logically.

A danger with using this multi-structure or multi-element format is that it can end up a bit disjointed if the writer isn't careful. Although the writer may have an entry point in mind for the story, the reader may decide to read some other element of the story first. In traditional newspaper writing, the reader had to follow the story line as the writer wrote it. Not so with the web. Therefore, it is critical that each chunk of information be complete in itself. Each segment should be in the inverted pyramid form and be able to stand on its own. And each segment may need to contain the basic elements of the overall story so the reader can understand the gist of the story regardless of which segment he's reading. This may mean some repetition, but the reader must be able to understand each sidebar in relation to the main story.

Communication, by definition, requires feedback. That means we really don't have complete communication until the sender hears back from the receiver. One of the shortcomings of traditional mass media systems — newspapers and broadcast — is that we often send out messages without knowing if they were received. Occasionally, someone might write a letter to the editor. Even then, it might be days or weeks later. It's one of the reasons journalists attempt to keep their messages simple — to better ensure that the message sent is the message received. In face-to-face conversations, this isn't a problem since the receiver can immediately tell the sender he didn't understand the message. With the time delay involved in most mass media systems, however, that's a problem.

The web has changed all that. Now the reader can immediately provide the writer with feedback, and that can add to the discussion or better enable the writer to clarify his message in subsequent reports. You just want to hear from your readers, however. So, change your email address from time to time to avoid unwanted spam.

Remember, web readers are in a hurry. They don't read the news as much as they scan the news, and they expect the stories to be interconnected, accurate, succinct, and to the point.

Perhaps the most widely-recognized example of an online reporting structure can be found on *Wikipedia*, the online encyclopedia website. It starts with a headline identifier of the subject (what journalists call the *lead*), follows with a paragraph or two of general information (what journalists call the *nut graph* defining the important elements of the story), and then proceeds to break the story into segments covering different topics of the story with a subhead announcing each section and imbedded links within the text referring the reader to other sources of information. It should be noted, however, that online story structures vary. Many still rely heavily on inverted pyramid structure.

• Exercise •

Review an online news site and show how the elements work together. Then give students the facts for a story and have them write the lead. Tell them to make sure the key words are in the lead so the search engine will be able to correctly identify the story for the reader. Have them write the rest of the story using the inverted pyramid. Once they have finished, tell them to write the story again using half as many words but not leaving out any of the facts.

Afterwards, provide them with the video, audio, still photographs, and graphics to the story and have them rewrite it, using subheads and internal and external links, and clumping the information and layering it into a complete package in which all the elements complement one another.

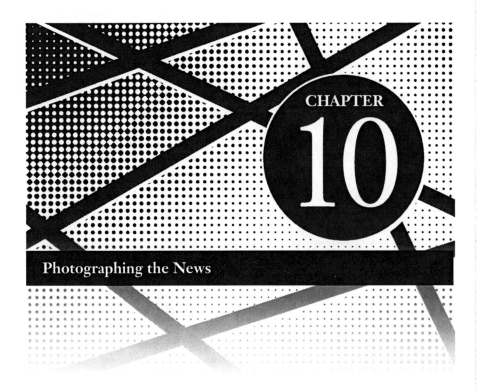

• The Photojournalist •

Reporting the news involves more than just writing stories. Pictures have always been a part of storytelling. Earliest man scratched his history on the walls of caves — not in words, but in images. Woodcuts and illustrative engravings were printed alongside words in newspapers long before the era of the photograph. Little wonder then that almost from the moment it was invented the camera has been an important tool in newsgathering.

Despite this, photographers and writers have always considered their roles to be separate. They worked together, but each required different training. Obviously, knowing how to write is not the same thing as knowing how to take pictures. In today's converged media, Internet world, however, things have changed. No longer can one go to school thinking they are going to take pictures and not write or write and not take pictures. All journalists must learn at least the basics of photojournalism in addition to mastering writing skills. They must learn to tell stories in a variety of ways.

A photojournalist is someone who tells stories with photographs. He's more than a photographer. A photographer takes pictures of nouns; a photojournalist takes pictures of verbs. When you tell a story with words you use nouns, verbs, and a direct object. News photography uses the same construction. Each photo must tell us what happened. It must be a complete thought. It must be a visual report of the facts.

Photojournalists, like all journalists, must be able to cover a variety of assignments, and they must be able to adapt their skills and personality to each situation. General news reporting requires them to be able to tell a complete story, often using a photo package utilizing different pictures. In sports photography they must show action, conflict, and emotion. Spot news requires them to be fast, bold, and even courageous. They may need to take portraits, capturing the essence of the person in his environment. Photojournalists must be able to read facial expressions. A tear, a smile, a glance shows the personality of the subject. They must be empathetic.

Good pictures require thought and planning. Photojournalists look for pictures that contain drama, action, and expression — in hands and other body parts as well as the face — and unusualness. They understand light and contrast. Natural light generated by nature will have a different effect on the photo than artificial light. Generally, natural light is preferred, though that's not always possible. Contrast, the difference between light and dark, can affect the way we see a picture. It can add drama or intrigue, and it can affect the interpretation of a picture. Darken a person's face and he looks guilty. Too much light and he appears ill.

• Basic Photocomposition Rules •

Good photojournalists, like good writers, understand the basic rules of their craft. They include the following:

Distance – How far are you from the subject? Most beginning photojournalists don't get close enough. Having said that, even beginning photographers understand that when it comes to distance there are three kinds of photos: long range, midrange, and close-up.

Long-range shots, often known as *establishing shots*, show a scene in its entirety. Long-range shots can give us an overall view of a situation so we can put things in context. If we're going to shoot a mountain climber, at some point we want to see the mountain he is going to climb.

Midrange shots are often used in sports photography. They focus on the subject but also provide some of the surroundings so we can figure out what is happening. Getting these pictures requires the photographer to move, change positions, and try to get the picture from a variety of angles. Good photographers look for interesting angles. They may need to lie down or climb up on something to get the shot they want.

Close-up shots require some guts. It means the photojournalist must be courageous enough to overcome his own comfort zone as well as his subject's and get in for the full frame picture that gives the detailed information about the subject.

Courtesy of Mark Zimmerman.

Courtesy of Mark Zimmerman.

Courtesy of Mark Zimmerman.

Proper orientation – How are you holding the camera? Will you get a horizontal shot or turn the camera on its side and get a vertical shot? Obviously a wide scene, such as a beach, is best shot with a horizontal orientation while a tall scene, such as a tree, is best shot vertically.

Courtesy of Mark Zimmerman.

Rule of thirds – This rule helps photographers compose shots in a more natural way and gets them away from centering every picture. It helps direct the viewer's eye to the important *Courtesy of Mark Zimmerman.* parts of the photo. It also helps them see things they might not otherwise see. It works by dividing the photo into nine equal parts. First, draw two vertical lines that divide the picture into three equal segments. Then do the same thing horizontally as if you were playing tic-tac-toe. Photographers will place the center of interest along the lines or wherever two lines intersect.

Courtesy of Mark Zimmerman.

Balance – The rule of thirds may make for a more interesting picture, but it can also cause it to be out of balance. Photographers will overcome this by including another lesser-important object where the void is. Obviously, you can't manipulate the content of the photo, but you can change angles to include other elements that are there.

Courtesy of Mark Zimmerman.

Lines – Our eyes are drawn naturally along the lines in a photo. If you photograph a curvy road, the viewer's eye will "travel" the road through the scene. Photos can have straight lines, diagonal lines, zigzag lines, all kinds of lines. The way you place them in your composition will affect the way the viewer sees the picture. It can pull him into it or move us through it like following a road.

Courtesy of Mark Zimmerman.

143

Patterns – Patterns or symmetry can make eye-catching photos.

Courtesy of Mark Zimmerman.

Viewpoint – Where will you stand (or sit or lie) to take the photo? It will change the viewpoint and the message you send. This involves more than just getting a long shot, a medium shot, or a close-up. The angle can change the background and what is emphasized in the picture.

Courtesy of Mark Zimmerman.

Background – What's behind the picture? Remember that when you take the photo you get more than the subject, you also get what's behind it. Try to find a background that won't distract from your subject. Taking a picture of someone standing in front of a palm tree might seem

Courtesy of Mark Zimmerman.

interesting, but it won't seem so great when you discover the tree is growing out of his head.

Depth – By including objects in the foreground and background or by overlapping one object partially with another, you can create depth.

Courtesy of Mark Zimmerman.

Framing – Look for objects that can frame your picture, such as trees and arches. It helps focus the viewer's eyes on the main subject of the picture.

Courtesy of Mark Zimmerman.

Cropping – Pull the reader closer to your subject by cutting off distracting elements along the sides of the picture. Better photographers will attempt to crop their photos when they first compose the shot instead of waiting later and discovering they didn't pull in close enough when they took the picture.

Courtesy of Mark Zimmerman.

Take lots of pictures – In the digital age, there's no reason not to shoot as many times as you want. You don't have to buy film anymore. Experiment with different angles, light, framing, etc. Chances are at least one of those shots will turn out right.

• Photo Editing •

Editing is as important in photography as it is in writing. Photo editing involves three basic procedures. The first is **selection**. Which photo do you use? News photos capture attention and illustrate editorial content. Editors look to see if the photo is dramatic. Does the picture tell a story? A photo of a twisted bicycle with someone crying nearby tells a story. Emotion is equally appealing. Put a puppy in the right picture and everyone's happy. News is action. Movement in any photo grabs the eye. The editor will also note the technical quality of the photo. Is it sharp and clear, properly lighted, and in focus? Has the photographer followed the basic rules of composition? Photos of unusual subjects or prominent people are eye-catchers. **Cropping**, as already noted, is another editing tool. To crop a photo is to take part of it away — the part that doesn't matter because it's unnecessary to the subject or because you want to eliminate parts that distract from the point of the picture. Cropping can enhance a photo by zeroing in on what's really important. Finally, the **size** of the photo will help define its importance. The bigger it is, the more attention it gets. In a picture story one photo should dominate because it best captures the essence of the story.

• Cutlines and Captions •

Just because you take pictures doesn't mean you don't have to write. Great photos still need cutlines to identify who is in the picture or explain what is going on in it. Consequently, all photojournalists must carry a pencil and notebook with them. Cutlines, which usually appear below the picture, identify, explain, and describe. They come in two forms: long *story* lines and short *skel* lines. Long lines are full explanations of the photo. They are mini stories that answer who, what, when, where, how, and why. They are used with photos that stand alone without an accompanying story. The trick is not to repeat what's in the photo but to reinforce or amplify it by putting it in context with other facts. Short lines may offer a name or one line. They are used with photos that accompany a story that fully explains the situation the photo describes. Therefore, we don't need to answer all the questions a story would. Cutlines should be written in present tense and be specific. All pictures should have cutlines and all names should be double-checked for accuracy.

Long lines of a stand-alone photo of cars driving through a flooded street in the wake of a hurricane might look like this:

> *Traffic slowly makes its way through the flooded streets of New Orleans Thursday in the wake of Hurricane Isaac, which dumped more than nine inches of rain on some parts of the city and caused six fatalities.*

Story lines often can include even more information.

Short lines of a photo of a roofer that accompanies a story about the perils of roofing houses in 100-degree heat would be brief:

> *Bobby Jones nails down a shingle with his empty water bottle in his pocket.*

• Picture Stories •

Picture stories use a variety of related photos to tell a story. The story must be able to be told visually. Picture stories should contain a **central idea** that, like any other story, can be stated in one sentence. **People** are usually the most important part of the story. Depending upon the situation, you may need to get their permission before shooting the project. **Location** is important. Again permission may be needed. Additionally, does it provide a dramatic setting? Can you get a variety of pictures and angles? Will the lighting be adequate? Stories involve **action**. Make sure you can position yourself well to capture it. Look for **expression and emotion**. They connect the viewer with the subject. Lastly, think how you will **order and lay out** the photos. Does the story involve a logical or chronological series of events?

• Audio Slideshows and Video •

Audio slideshows and video marry pictures to sound. This marriage, like all marriages, requires careful scripting. Nevertheless, the advent of the Internet has made this format for storytelling increasingly important. Check the websites for the major news organizations and you will find examples of how it's done.

As with picture stories, you want to include a variety of photos clearly depicting a central idea. In fact, the same techniques used in picture stories will be used here. Think of the story having a beginning, middle, and end. Obviously, in the beginning you want to introduce the topic, then expand on it in the body much the same way a broadcast story unfolds.

Often the sound portion of the package merely consists of the reporter talking into the microphone. It's better if this is scripted and practiced. It should also be written for the ear. The photographer should use short words and simple sentences and read it aloud to make sure it is clear to the listener the first time through. Most slideshows last from two to three minutes. Make sure what is being described matches the picture being shown and that those pictures that need more explanation are timed correctly and don't spill over into the next photograph.

Slideshows come in two forms. In one, the audio is continuous without pausing as the photos change. These work if the pictures don't require individual explanation. The audio matches the photos but does not refer to each picture. The second form matches the audio to each picture and changes only after each photo has been explained. The audio in either form can include sounds other than voices, including music and sounds of nature. To marry the pictures to the words, use a broadcast script or format it so the words are on the left half of the page and the photo and the time (in seconds) to show it are on the right side. The time it takes to read it should match the time it takes to show it.

• Photo Ethics •

Photography offers its own unique set of ethical problems. Most usually involve two main issues: **interference** and **manipulation**. A photojournalist must never direct or pose subjects unless it's for a portrait, and then it must be noted in the caption. Staging news photos is strictly forbidden.

Neither should the photojournalist alter what's in the photo. This is true also during editing. Cropping is okay, unless it misleads, but taking wrinkles off the face, or moving objects in or out or around a picture, or using artistic license for dramatic effect is wrong. The photojournalist is trying to give a picture of reality, and only those actions — correcting for color, exposure, sharpness, etc. — that help present that reality are appropriate.

Pictures can lie. They don't show everything the eye can see. Their focus is selected and narrow. They can't show context or what comes before or after. They can, therefore, be misleading. Nevertheless, we tend to believe what we see. So the journalist must be careful what he shows. To this end, photojournalists should be accurate and comprehensive, avoid bias and stereotype, treat subjects with respect and dignity, and refuse gifts or favors from those who seek to influence coverage. Neither should they pay for news or engage in criminal behavior to get their photos.

It should be noted that photojournalists should be sensitive to those situations involving grief, embarrassment, children, and sex. And they should not intrude on private moments unless there is an overriding and justifiable public interest — a need to know, not just a want to know.

• Exercise •

Take pictures incorporating each of the basic composition rules listed above. Write full story lines for one.

CHAPTER

11

Feature Writing

Reprinted by permission of Dr. Terry M. Clark.

• Purpose •

Structure is everything to effective feature writing, after excellent reporting. In fact, you have to be a better reporter to write feature stories than most straight news stories because you're writing about the people and ideas and events behind the news. And you're no longer telling; you're showing.

So what's a feature story? And how do you write one?

First, there's no simple answer, other than *human interest story*. Except instead of listing the facts in inverted pyramid order, features are told much the same way people traditionally tell stories, with a beginning, middle, and end.

Feature stories are a regular staple of both print and broadcast journalists and can cover a variety of topics.

- **News features** – One of the two most common in deadline journalism. A human-interest story related to a recent news event, going beyond the news and showing the impact or effects of the event on people.
- **Personality profiles** – Telling the story of interesting people, or of people retiring.
- **How-to stories** – Explaining how to build an airplane in your garage or help your children deal with bullying.
- **Historical features** – Picking out local attractions or anniversaries and finding local people to tell the story from a local angle.
- **Travel stories** – These fill the travel sections of newspapers and travel magazines, telling about trips and travel tips.
- **Information pieces** – Explaining the process behind something complicated, or telling a story about a local business or enterprise.
- **Obituaries** – A good obituary is essentially a feature story about a person's life, with funeral information and survivors added. See them in *The New York Times*.

Where do you get ideas for feature stories — assuming an editor didn't assign one? As CBS journalist Charles Kuralt said, "Roll down the window and look."

To be a feature writer, to write human interest stories, you have to be a student of your readers and their interests, and a student, an observer, of what people are interested in. Every feature story starts with curiosity about something. In fact, if you or someone else says, "I wonder about..." chances are there is a feature story to answer the question.

• First Step – The Idea •

Writing a feature story is a fluid five-step process. You don't start writing when you sit down to the computer. The writing begins with the idea. Every story starts with an angle, the reason for writing the story and the approach you take to do it.

If you live in a town with a military base and the editor tells you to go do a story on the veteran in the wheelchair protesting the war, you've already started writing. Now you start formulating your questions and the direction of your story. The angle is obviously the tension, the contrast of an anti-war veteran in a military town.

You are not ready to continue writing until you can complete the following sentence: This is a story about (a veteran in a wheel chair) and it is interesting because (he's protesting the war in a town where most of my readers are military).

This sentence is the most important one you will write. It saves you time later and becomes your theme statement. It may change after you continue reporting and writing, but it gives your story focus. Eventually, it will become part of your *nut graph* that tells the reader what the story is about. It also helps you focus your questions for interviews.

• Second Step – Reporting, Research •

Reporting is the second step of writing, which is why interviewing is so critical to the feature writer. Almost all feature stories have people in them as sources and subjects. Your ability to report and tell a story will depend in a large part on your ability to get your sources to talk.

That means open-ended questions, questions that put your subjects at ease, questions that encourage them to speak freely. Remember, you're not asking so much for straight facts, but trying to get the why and how behind those facts — what is inside your subject's mind and heart.

You'll also be noting the appearance of the subject, the environment, gestures, anything that helps show the subject. In feature writing, you're trying to put flesh onto the bones of the subject.

• Third Step – Organization •

This is the area most journalists ignore in the rush to deadline. They sit down and start typing. In news, the inverted pyramid's formula makes this easy, and when the contents of the notebook have been dumped into the computer, most important to least, they stop typing and hit the "submit" key.

But feature writing is different than writing about news events, because you have to grab your readers' attention and lure them into the story. That's why the structure of a feature story is so important.

Essentially, you're asking your reader for a date — a date with their time and interest. The organization of a feature story is the same as a date. Catch the person's attention — *the wink*, ask for the date, go on the date, and save something for a goodnight kiss to conclude the story.

Just as writing the theme statement saves you time, so will making this simple outline, with a few key words in each area before you start "writing."
- The wink – catch their attention (the lead)
- Ask for the date – nut graph
- Go on the date – rest of story
- The goodnight kiss – conclusion

Another approach is to organize your story into scenes, like a movie. The most dramatic is the first scene. It leads to the next, and builds up the action. Think of a recent TV commercial, for instance. Save a good scene for the conclusion. Scene by scene organization is like advertising storyboarding. The power of scene-by-scene construction is that each scene usually involves a character or characters, scene setting (description), and action and suspense to keep you interested until the next scene.

William Blundell, who wrote for the *Wall Street Journal*, recommended you take your theme statement and tape it to the computer monitor in front of you to help you organize and write your story.

• Fourth Step – Writing •

Before you begin, remember to type your story without looking at your notes. That way, you'll only include the information that really sticks in your memory. Once you've done that, then go back, fill in the blanks and details and facts you need to ensure accuracy and completeness.

First, catch your reader's attention. This is your lead, the wink that entices the reader. Catching people's attention may take more than a few words, depending on the subject. Start with an interesting lead that emphasizes people or the subject. Best test for a good lead — do I want to keep reading? Use the most compelling information you've gathered. Go for the drama. Think of the last movie you saw, and the scene that opened it. That's what you're trying to do. You want people in action, or description that fits the overall sense of the story. If this is a feature story related to a recent news event, it may only be a sentence or two. For a profile or something else, it may be several sentences.

Now you take your theme statement — "This is a story about... and it's interesting because" and rewrite it in story form to become your nut graph, what the story is about. This is essentially a who, what, when, where, why, and how standard news lead: *John Jones, a decorated Vietnam War vet, parks his wheelchair in front of the gate to Tinker Air Base every day, protesting the war in Afghanistan.*

Take the rest of your material, and outline it in two or three major blocks of related information, organizing from most compelling and important to the least. Then tell the rest of the story, including quotes from key people, some description, and other information. But as with a date, choose a plan carefully, and don't bore your date with haphazard and long-winded conversation. Start out with the most pertinent information to the angle of the story. In the story about the protesting vet, that would be his reasons and emotions, the why behind his actions. Since it's a profile, save most of the biographical history for a couple of sentences or paragraphs late in the story. On the vet, this would be where he went to school, what his other jobs have been, and so on.

Don't put the entire contents of your notebook in or you will put your readers to sleep. Nobody likes long sermons, or windy articles, either. Instead, select the best parts, and then pay attention to organizing the story to attract and keep the readers' attention.

Now it's time for the goodnight kiss. Save something to leave a sweet taste in the reader's mouth and mind. This might be your second best quote, or other material that ties back to the material you used in the lead, emphasizing what the story is about.

Here's an example from Terry Clark's 2011 story in *Persimmon Hill* magazine:

- **Theme statement written ahead of time:** *This is a story about Bob Pickering and his talk about the image of the bison at the Prix de West show, and it's interesting because of his viewpoint and the audience.*

- **Start with a crisp lead:** *The power of the bison is still there today,* said Dr. Robert B. Pickering, speaking to the morning crowd at the 37th annual Prix de West weekend on *The Image of the Bison.*
- **Nut graph** (re-written theme statement): *Pickering, senior curator of the Gilcrease Museum in Tulsa and director of a new Museum science program at Tulsa University, led the audience through the history of the bison in art, but not from an artist's viewpoint.*
- **Story and quote:** *I'm looking at the bison as depicted. Are these representations useful as historic records?* Pickering said. He focused...
- **Conclusion:** *The buffalo is one of the most interesting creatures on the continent, affecting ecology, history, human culture,* Pickering said. *It is powerful physically, magically, spiritually, and became the symbol, the icon of the American West.*

• Fifth Step – Revising, Editing •

Just because you've finished typing and run out of notes doesn't mean you're through writing. If you have time, let the story sit for a night, and get up and work on improving it after you've let it stew in your head a little. If you don't have that much time, walk away from it for an hour, and come back.

Check your spelling. Check the facts. Check AP style. Have I paragraphed often enough? Do the quotes all begin new paragraphs? Is there a better lead? What can I cut out that will improve the story? Is there anything else I need to include? Read the story out loud to yourself. That highlights problems. Print the story on paper, and go through it with a pen and pencil.

"All writing is selection," says master non-fiction writer John McPhee. Feature writers have to be experts at selecting not just details, facts, and description, but in choosing what will be included in the lead to the story — the most important sentences in the story.

That's because the lead must capture the readers' attention and make them want to keep reading past the first few sentences. So the writer, the student of his readers' interests, is always looking for the details, the quotes, the material that do that while integral to the subject and tone of the story.

Go for the drama. What you want to do in the first few sentences is create a scene involving action or people, perhaps with a note of suspense, mystery, or conflict, if possible.

Consider the first two sentences of the case study at the end of the chapter. The suspense is created because the reader has to keep reading to answer what and where.

Essentially there are three kinds of leads, with the lines between them blurred, that feature writers use to try to set these scenes.

Anecdotal/situational – These are preferred for grabbing attention because they are small stories and scenes, usually involving people in action. There are two kinds of anecdotes — on site and narrated. If you're doing a profile on a retiring police officer and he tells you an interesting story about shooting himself in the foot, you might start with a quote from him and describe the situation. If it's something you observe as a writer, you might start with *The long thin fingers of the frustrated pianist work the switches on the control panel....*

Try to show the subject in relation to the main interest point in the story. Give the reader a character, or characters, to identify with. Put the character in action and let the reader see it all by providing description. Make the lead create a specific incident or scene or sense.

Descriptive – This is the second best way to start a story, as long as the description is brief and vivid, concentrating on key elements. The OU Press story at the end of this chapter has elements of this.

Essay – This is the weakest way to start a feature story. It's essentially term paper writing without footnotes, and nobody, but old English teachers perhaps, reads term papers for fun. *Classical music at KCSC radio station is more interesting than one might imagine.*
Yawn.

There are easy ways to build suspense and drama in your leads. Use mystery nouns or pronouns in the first few sentences, or unexplained reactions. We have to keep reading to find out which pianist the fingers belong to. Short paragraphs and sentences also help create suspense.
And keep the lead short as well.

Next, pay attention to the tools as you're going through the story again. Feature writers use many so-called fiction techniques, but they're really just tools in a toolbox — as Stephen King would call them — for telling a story. William Blundell said that the first commandment for a feature writer is: "Tell me a story and make it interesting." Understand that mastering these tools are essential building blocks for crafting a story people will want to read. To effectively tell an interesting story, your tools must involve verbs, quotes, description, and effective paragraphs.

While the first sentence of the story is the most important, the most important words in that sentence, and in every sentence you write as a journalist and storyteller, are verbs. Without verbs, nothing happens. Nouns and adverbs and adjectives sit like empty boxcars on a siding, going nowhere, without a locomotive. Without verbs, there aren't sentences to express thoughts. Without them, you can't tell anybody what happened. Verbs are crucial to grabbing and keeping readers' attention. Specific verbs add description, like *gurgled* or *tumbled*.

Verbs carry the energy of your sentences. All successful writers pay attention to verbs, emphasizing active voice and action verbs, because they enliven writing. They seek ways to avoid passive verbs (is, are, was, were) as much as possible. Passive verbs are easy to write, as in this sentence, but make for wordier, stale writing devoid of movement. Movement is the key to storytelling. The verb in your sentences empowers your sentences. Don't weigh them down and weaken them with fat (extra words). Simplify — get rid of the *had been decided* or *having been voted on* or *have missed* and write *decided, voted,* and *missed*.

That's also why we use *said* for all attribution. No other words are needed, not *repeated, laughed* (technically impossible), *remembered*, etc.

Before you start composing the story, make a list of the active verbs you think you might use. This will help you use more active voice verbs and enliven your writing. And when you run spell-check, turn on the readability feature that gives you percentage of passive verbs. If it's more than 25 percent, revise.

Use quotes. Research shows that readers' eyes will skip other writing and go to the quotes. Direct quotes are the eye-contact of writing, grabbing the reader's attention, and giving humanity to your writing. How can you have a human-interest story if people are not talking in it? In fiction, it's called *dialogue.* That's not the long, PR-government-educational official quotes, but the ones that come from inside a person's heart. Jesus said, "from out of the abundance of the heart the mouth speaks." Tom Wolfe said that nothing gets us closer to what a person is really like than realistic dialogue.

It's your job to get your subjects talking, or people talking about your subject, and to capture those snippets that grab attention, that explain better than any long prose the essence of what you're writing about. Good feature writers dig for quotes, mine for them, using a backhoe or a shovel to scoop out information with open-ended questions. Sometimes they'll be found within a longer quote, and it's your job to cut away the fat and just use the lean sinew that has power. Also, if a good quote is buried inside a longer quote that's essential, use the interesting part in quotes and paraphrase the rest, because you can write it more concisely that way. As long as you don't change the context, there's no harm. Example, *Quotes are the eye contact of writing,* he said, claiming you can't write a feature story...

Most feature stories should have a quote within the first few paragraphs, if the story doesn't start with one, which is effective in a profile. Do not bury the quotes inside a paragraph. Start a new paragraph with the quote, followed by the attribution.

Use description. Joseph Conrad said, "above all, I want to make you see."

Feature writers attempt to show readers, rather than tell them. Good storytellers paint pictures in their readers' minds with words. That's why feature writers employ effective description to grab and keep readers' attentions. Pretend your story won't appear with a photograph; description shows your readers the subject.

Description involves appealing to the readers' senses, telling about smells, sights, sounds, tastes, touches, words of color. You do this by including specific details, specific action verbs, and fresh imagery — metaphors and similes — to paint pictures in their minds. Don't write, *It was a noisy, beat up truck.* Write: *The battered 1956 Ford pickup rattled down the highway, sounding like a tin can full of rocks.* For effective use of similes and metaphors, study the parables of Jesus.

George Orwell, in *Politics and the English Language,* had this test for writers: "A scrupulous writer, in every sentence that he writes, will ask himself at least four questions, thus:
- "What am I trying to say?"
- "What words will best express it?"
- "What image or idiom will make it clearer?"
- "Is this image fresh enough to have an effect?"

Finally, check your paragraphs. Long blocks of gray type lose readers quickly because their eyes get tired and they keep hoping to skip to the next main idea. Eventually, they get lost in all the words and different thoughts and start scanning to speed up, or just quit reading.

Paragraph often and vary the length of them so the short ones provide emphasis between the longer ones. You will rarely have a paragraph of more than three sentences. Stephen King wrote in *On Writing,* that paragraphs are important for the way they look on a page. That's especially true for journalists.

• Case Study •

The following story started with "I wonder."

Research began with a visit to the subject's web page, which had lots of facts, and then emails and phone calls to set up interviews. The theme statement became, *This is a story about the OU Press, which is interesting because most Oklahomans don't know about it, and it has an international reputation for publishing books on Native Americans.* It was necessary to visit the place for interviews and descriptive visits.

The paragraphs are numbered for reference. Paragraphs one and two are the wink. Three and four are the nut graph, adapted from the theme statement. Twenty and twenty-one are the good night kiss, tying back to the first two paragraphs. Note the description and verbs in paragraphs two, seven, and seventeen. The goal is to walk the reader through the press, and get a feel for its atmosphere and understand its operation.

"Pressing On," From *Oklahoma Today*, July/August 2012 by Terry M. Clark. Copyright © 2012 by *Oklahoma Today*. Reprinted by permission.

1. A yellowed 1941 first edition of Angie Debo's *The Road to Disappearance* leans against a 1979 paperback reprint of the famous Oklahoman's history of the Creek Nation.

2. The masterpieces crowd floor-to-ceiling shelves packed with about 4,500 different books in a little-known Norman library. Walk into the 14-foot by 25-foot room, spread your hand over the volumes on every wall, and you'll touch more books about Indians.

3. "We're known as 'The Cowboy and Indian Press' for a reason," says B. Byron Price, director of the University of Oklahoma Press. The room holds every book the press has published since it was founded in 1928, and a third of them are about Native Americans, Price says.

4. Today, the press publishes almost 80 fine-quality books a year as its role and international reputation in Native American publishing is expanding.

5. "There's a tremendous interest in Native American cultures. Our books help clarify cultures that have been sometimes misrepresented in the past, and they represent the vitality of those cultures today," Price says.

6. He rattles off names of current books and authors like they were his children. "A book should engage your senses," he says, rubbing the glossy cover of one volume. "It is important how a book looks and feels — the quality should be comparable to the quality of the content."

7. Charles Rankin, editor-in-chief, works in an office cluttered with manuscripts, a Jerome Tiger print of the Trail of Tears on the wall, one of Custer's Last Stand propped on the floor. He and three other acquisitions editors sift an average of about five proposals each [and] every week, ranging from subjects on Indians to the classics, military history and football.

8. "But if the OU Press stands on two pillars, they are Native American studies, which led to the American West," Rankin says. "That's our essence."

9. Rankin says the press has formed partnerships with the Chickasaw and Cherokee presses as a distributor. It teams with art museums like the Gilcrease, Philbrook, and Joslyn to produce books on Native American art. It works with students in a unique Ph.D. program in Native American art at the OU Art School.

10. Authors like C. Blue Clark, OCU law professor who wrote *Indian Tribes of Oklahoma–A Guide* (2009), praise the demanding editorial standards leading to the high quality of OU Press books.

11. Quality brings national awards. "The awards are the gravy," says Price. There's a lot of gravy — more than 240 national awards in 10 years. A display case in the front window alone holds three National Cowboy and Western Heritage Museum Wrangler Awards for non-fiction.

12. For a university press, it is mid-sized, 29 employees, with a $3-4 million budget supplemented by major grants for what Price calls "landmark" works. But the OU Press doesn't own a press, working with several printers across the country and overseas.

13. The best seller is *The Sacred Pipe*, (1953) with 125,000 sales, says Dale Bennie, marketing director, and that's from multiple printings. Most press runs are only about 1,200, but the OU Press is not a small business. It processes about 2,300 orders a month, netting more than $3 million in revenue a year.

14. "We have a book list as deep as anyone in America," he says, noting the 28 active book series, including the longest, the "Civilization of the American Indian" with more than 250 titles.

15. Bennie turns to twin computer screens and tells you how many copies of any book — hardback, paperback, or now e-book — have been sold. He's proud of repeat sales like Roger Nichols' 2004 *Indian Tribes in U.S. History* used as [a] school textbook every year.

16. Another top seller is Kingsley Bray's 2006 *Crazy Horse*, with 9,500 in hardback, 4,000 in paperback — edging into the e-book sales.

17. In a cavernous three-story-tall red brick warehouse of the OU Press facing I-35 in Norman, one million books in cartons fill metal shelves soaring to the ceiling. Just east of there, the library and offices occupy the front of a 20,000 square-foot metal building. In the back is the "Pick and Pack" shipping area, shelves lined with more than 2,500 different book titles ready to be shipped around the world.

18. Rankin sees a strong future. "We are blessed with an abundance of good material and recruiting possibilities. With 500 tribes, Indians are as strong as they've ever been."

19. In 2005 it acquired the Arthur Clark imprint, publisher of more than 600 books about the West. It is moving into e-book sales, and books about indigenous people in Central and South America. The website www.oupress.com is sophisticated, but user friendly.

20. About every six weeks, Rankin, Price, and the rest of the editorial committee sit down at the conference table in the library to consider new books that may one day sit on the shelves surrounding them.

21. "We're building on what is naturally Oklahoma," Price says of the Native American books. "It's a testimony to what we're about."

• Exercise •

Suppose today's news carries a story about Steve Smith, a teen-age swimmer, legally blind since birth, who rescued a drowning boy, Jake Jones, yesterday in a local lake. Your job is to write a news feature on him the next day.

- **Step one:** Write the theme sentence: "This is a story about...."
- **Step two:** In your interview with him and from the news story, you have his parents' names, his age, where he goes to school, how long he's been a swimmer, what his plans for the future are, including hoping for the Olympics. He's a member of the high school swim team. He's going to get a state award for saving the boy. You have some description of him — tanned, muscular, sandy hair. He wears goggles when swimming, sunglasses the other times. He learned to swim about the time he learned to walk. You learn the boy's cries for help and the yells of people on the shore helped guide him to the boy. He tells you, "I love swimming. I'd almost rather be able to swim than see." "It was easy to find the boy, because I could feel his frantic vibrations in the water. It was like I could see him."
- **Step three:** List at least four important open-ended questions to ask.
- **Step four:** List at least five of the action verbs you think you might use in the story.
- **Steps five and six:** Organize and write the story. What will be your lead sentence? Rewrite your theme statement into the nut graph. What will you save for the conclusion? Make up the facts you need for a 300-word story.

This is a news feature so the lead is going to be one or two sentences, and the nut graph will refer back to the news event.

CHAPTER

12

Writing the Depth/Investigative Story

• Making a Difference •

The ultimate power of the Press resides in two basic kinds of stories — the depth story and the investigative story. More than just telling us the news, they endeavor to explain complex things in detail and ferret out evil, inefficiency, and corruption.

By shining a light in dark places, they show us society's flaws and rally public opinion to challenge the status quo, to right wrongs, and hold those in power accountable. In the hands of skilled journalists they can literally strike fear in the hearts and minds of the most powerful people on earth. And they can change law and the course of society as surely as government itself.

Crusading journalism has been with us from even before the American Revolution when John Peter Zenger dared speak out against political corruption in New York. And it has served as a reflection of the American conscience ever since. In the early twentieth century Ida Tarbell exposed the country's oil monopoly — an effort that earned her and other crusading journalists at the time the title of *muckrakers* by President Theodore Roosevelt. Later, Upton Sinclair exposed the horrors of the early meatpacking industry. And later still, Bob Woodward and Carl Bernstein of *The Washington Post* told us of corruption in the highest office in the land — bringing down a president in the process.

Depth and investigative stories represent the most important work in journalism, but they are also the most difficult to do, and only the most experienced journalists are usually assigned to do them. They require intelligence, courage, and tenacity.

With the demise of many big city daily newspapers, some have suggested these stories may be a thing of the past because in addition to time and talent, they also take money and the backing of a powerful news organization with lawyers at the ready. But various nonprofit organizations around the country working mostly online have taken up the challenge. Whether they will be as successful remains to be seen. It takes a powerful Press to watch over a powerful government and business community.

Ironically, the Internet, which is in some ways responsible for the dwindling number of newspapers, has given reporters a valuable new tool in exchange to help them with their investigations. Computerized research has made gathering and analyzing data faster and easier. Surveys, charts, and diagrams can be done in hours instead of days or weeks. And as more information becomes available online, reporters will find that a few can now do the work of many.

• Differences and Similarities Between Depth and Investigative Stories •

Depth stories and investigative stories have much in common. They are both long and exhaustive, focus on details, and endeavor to explain complex subjects. In a sense, the word *investigative* applies to both since both are about investigating something.

But the depth story does not focus on things that people are trying to keep hidden. It is not concerned with finding wrongdoing. The depth story's job is to explain a complicated subject in such a way that everyone can understand it. Often these stories take up an entire page or section, or they may run in a series over several days or weeks. Many deal with science or technology. They may explain the mysteries of space or the intricacies of the human brain. They show how and why things happen and follow processes, start to finish, of complicated subjects. Most of the time they sound like long feature stories with lots of details.

The purpose of the investigative story, on the other hand, is to investigate and expose society's problems. The Press has no police power of its own. Instead, it uses its ability to publicize and embarrass. As angry citizens and consumers learn of problems, they demand correction and change.

As noted earlier, the investigative story is not a story about how the district attorney or the police are investigating something; it is when the news organization itself, using its own resources of time, money, and people, investigate and expose problems. These stories, too, may run in a series over days or weeks.

Investigative stories are harder to do than depth stories and more dangerous. Reporters are sometimes met with death threats. The news organizations may be faced with lawsuits charging libel. Yet without these kinds of crusading stories corruption and inefficient government would prevail.

Depth stories are usually identifiable only by their length and detail, whereas news organizations will often announce in the beginning paragraph when the story is an investigative story. It is a badge of honor for the news organization. It shows the public the news organization is looking out for the community and pursuing the public good. These are the kinds of stories that build news organizations' reputations and reporters' careers.

• Researching the Depth and Investigative Story •

News stories usually come from breaking news events. But the depth story often starts with a scientific discovery or a perceived trend in society that requires a detailed analysis to understand. Sometimes it begins because the reporter simply wonders about how something works and commences to find out. Remember, these stories are usually about why or how.

The investigative story, however, usually begins with a tip from a source or a citizen that something needs correcting. It may be an allegation that a politician is taking bribes or that police are dealing narcotics. Or it may be that the reporter is suspicious about something from his own observations. Perhaps he's noticed from his daily review of police reports an increase in the number of accidents at a local amusement park. His newsman's instinct tells him to find out the reasons for the increase.

Still, the tip may or may not be true; the story may or may not be there. So the reporter must do some initial investigation to see if there is a story. This may take several days. If he finds that there may be a story, he needs to define from his initial inquiry what the story is likely to be. He also needs to decide if he can get the story. It doesn't do much good if you think you've found wrongdoing but can't prove it.

If he feels confident that there's a story and he can get it, he starts with a working hypothesis, just as a scientist would. And he should be able to state what it is, just as every reporter must be able to say, "My story is about…" Nevertheless, the journalist must be open to let the facts take him where the story goes and not force it to go where he thinks it should go. The idea is to find the truth, wherever it leads.

Think of it this way: the reporter finds an errant thread, wonders about it, and then pulls it as long as he can and as far as he can to see where it goes. Often reporters think the story is about one thing, only to find out that it develops into something else. Sometimes it develops into nothing at all.

The next step is to organize a plan of attack. Depth and investigative pieces are difficult because they involve gathering huge amounts of information. The journalist must figure out how to organize his investigation, what sources he needs to contact and where he needs to go first, second and third. Generally speaking, it's usually best to start close to home. The first person to consult is the editor. Other journalists in the newsroom may also be able to provide guidance or sources. As with any other story, the news library is an important starting point.

Most large stories require the aid of at least an editor to brainstorm questions, identify people and documents to pursue, and help organize the final story. Although depth stories do not involve the difficulty and intrigue of investigative pieces, they are nevertheless daunting tasks given the large amount of information that must be organized, so the help of a good editor is also invaluable.

It's important to figure out ahead of time how to organize information collected during the investigation. Some writers organize their information by topic or source and place it in individual files. Each reporter must be well organized and know how he's going to keep track of things as the story progresses. These techniques vary from journalist to journalist.

All interview notes should be labeled with the name of the source, their contact information, and the time, date, and place of the interview. Sensitive interviews should be recorded and the recordings cataloged. A source's allegations of wrongdoing should be confirmed by at least two independent sources. Confidential sources should be given a code name to disguise them. This way the name of the source will remain secret even if the material is subpoenaed.

It's also a good idea to keep the editor up-to-date on everything that happens and where everything is located in case something happens to the reporter. Years ago I knew an investigative reporter who fell overboard as he sailed alone to the Bahamas. The editors weren't aware of his plans and spent weeks with the police trying to figure out if he had been killed. His body was never found, but investigators concluded it was an accident. Investigative reporters, more than their counterparts, need to keep in close contact with their editors.

Generally, it's best to sit down with the editor and write out a plan of how to pursue the story. This will give order to the investigation and provide everyone with an idea of how long it might take to do the story. Understand, however, that all large stories take unexpected turns and encounter frequent delays.

Such a plan might look like this:

1. Write the hypothesis statement.
2. Note the sources, starting with the most important and identifying what each source can contribute.
3. Identify what documents are likely needed and how to get them. Which ones are public and open and which ones are not?

4. Organize questions for each source.
5. List the roadblocks one is likely to encounter. Who will be difficult and why?
6. Note any outside help needed. Will graphs, charts, surveys, photos, etc., be used? Who will provide them? What will they add to the story?
7. List a cost analysis of the project and identify needed purchases.
8. Identify publication dates. Will it be a one-day story/package or a series?
9. Note the prospects for follow-up stories.
10. List the order of the interviews and when to get documents. (The order in which information is received can be crucial and determine if the story is successful or not.)
11. Review information and organize related facts into story subtopics.
12. Outline the story structure, including lead and ending.
13. Write the story.
14. Review the story with the editor. (The reporter will work with the editor throughout the process.)
15. Have the legal department review the story.
16. Revise and rewrite.

Above all, the reporter must be paranoid about accuracy. Mistakes in a depth or investigative story are fatal to careers and pocketbooks. Suggest someone committed a crime when they didn't and the reporter is looking at a libel suit.

Some large stories require the work of more than one journalist. Some stories are so big they require the help of the entire news department. Such stories usually involve disasters. A case in point is the bombing of the Oklahoma City Federal Building in April 1995. Editors at *The Oklahoman* made use of every staff member. The newspaper divided up its staff and assigned reporters different aspects of the bombing to cover as editors worked to coordinate the project. The newspaper provided its staff with food and even professional psychological support to help them cope with covering the horror.

• Sources •

As with any other story, reporters should choose their sources carefully. They must be credible and knowledgeable. The reporter must know what each source will be able to contribute to the story or to the process. Some sources will be for attribution. Others will merely help the reporter find the sources he needs. All of the skills described in the chapter on interviewing come into play. The reporter needs to be able to think outside the box, to find sources in unlikely or unusual places. He will know and cultivate sources at the top of the social scale as well as those at the bottom. He will know ministers and murderers.

Reporters find sources by making a list. If they're doing a story on the police chief, they will note his enemies as well as his friends and colleagues. If the reporter finds information he doesn't understand — whether from people or documents, it will be necessary to find an expert to interpret it. All journalists cultivate and maintain sources with expertise in a variety of areas.

Victims can provide anecdotes and examples. Reporters must be on guard, however, with sources that may be looking for revenge. Their credibility may be tainted. Other sources may include people who may be caught in the middle between powerful forces and fear they may get hurt or lose something valuable — like their careers.

Documents, too, are important. Unlike people who may change their story, documents provide black and white evidence. A paper trail is usually more credible than a people trail. Ultimately, most investigative journalists look for some kind of written proof to back up their stories. Such evidence is usually more credible in court.

However, documents can be misconstrued unless the reporter has access to someone who can interpret them. Consequently, when the reporter finds the records, he also needs to find someone who can back them up. Records by themselves aren't very useful in court. Someone has to testify to their authenticity and meaning.

Documents can include business records — including records of incorporation, annual reports and Internal Revenue Service reports, campaign financial statements, minutes of meetings, and thousands of other kinds of documents. By the time the reporter is accomplished and experienced enough to do investigative journalism, he should have amassed a great deal of knowledge about government and business. He should know the various federal, state, and local agencies and departments, their leaders and procedures, what they control, and what records they have. He should have cultivated sources in these areas, including secretaries and clerks as well as managers and department heads.

Although knowing people is the best way to find information, occasionally the reporter may need to use the force of law to get what he needs. Most states have open meeting and open records laws to help citizens get information. The federal government, too, has laws that aid the reporter, including the Freedom of Information Act. These laws, however, should be used as a last resort. Many of them, including FOI, have long time-consuming procedures to follow and exempt much information from review.

Remember that politicians and business leaders generally have built protective fences around themselves. Secretaries and public relations people often work to keep reporters at bay. Consequently, journalists must often be creative in getting what they need. Remember that very little information is privy to only one person. Think of your most private information. Chances are someone else knows it. If a reporter can't get the information from one source, he should go around the corner and learn to get it from someplace or someone else. Be careful, however, not to break the law getting it.

• Writing the Depth and Investigative Story •

Organizing and telling the depth and investigative story can be overwhelming. Although the inverted pyramid may work, more often than not reporters must use a story structure that is peculiar to the information they've gathered. Each story then often comes with it's own unique structure and organizational problems. Consequently, the reporter, as with any other story, must look to the information he has gathered to determine how best to tell his story. Remember, the journalist's job is to lead the reader logically and clearly through a complex maze of information. The reader must understand what's going on every step of the way.

To begin, the reporter must go through his information to see how it naturally clumps together into related areas. He should put the related information together then organize it by topic and subtopic. Afterwards, it's important for him to list what he's got and then outline it in some pattern that the reader can follow. Most of the time, complex stories are compartmentalized, organizing chunks of information and presenting them in some logical or chronological manner.

Structurally, the story will contain many of the same elements as a feature story, including a lead, the nut graph explaining the point of the story, and a formal conclusion that may offer suggestions from experts about how to solve the problem noted in the story. In the middle, however, the story will focus more on explaining the various parts of the investigated problem or depth subject, noting consequences, critics' comments, rebuttals, and solutions.

Here is an example of a depth/investigative story structure:

1. Lead with an example or anecdote showing the problem and its effects.
2. Show the underlying cause with a one-sentence explanation of the reasons for the problem.
3. Write the nut graph using a paragraph summary of the basic elements and giving the reader an indication of what the story is about and the point of view it takes.
4. Explain the problem or parts of the story, using examples, statistics, experts, etc. This is the bulk of the story. If it's an investigative story, focus also on the following five elements.
5. Show the consequences of the problem.
6. Offer rebuttals from critics.
7. Answer the critics with additional facts from experts.
8. If left unsolved, show where the problem is likely to lead.
9. Give possible solutions.
10. Conclude the story with an example or anecdote of what will happen if the problem is left unsolved. In the case of the depth story, leave the reader with a picture of the subject of the story and how it works.

If the information doesn't lend itself to one story, the reporter should consider organizing it into separate stories. Is it possible to relate some of the information using charts or graphs or photos? Using these elements can help break up long passages of gray type as well as explain complex matters. Often complex stories are really complex packages. This is where the editor can help.

Given the complexity of most depth and investigative stories, the reporter must always be on guard against falling into complicated jargon. Neither should he print everything he knows. He should select the information that tells the story completely. And he should write each sentence simply. At the same time, however, he must be careful not to take things out of context or oversimplify them to where they are no longer accurate.

Attribution must be clear and constant. Every piece of information must be checked for accuracy and written and put in context within the story. Even accurate facts out of context can present legal problems. To add to the credibility, the editor should write a separate boxed notice to the reader and include it on the page with the story, explaining why and how the story was reported. An explanation of the methodology helps the reader follow your thinking process.

Remember that the reporter must be fair and objective in his reporting — seeking information that will lead him and his readers to the truth, but this does not mean he has to be neutral. The point of the investigative story is to point out wrongdoing. The muckrakers of the last century sought to expose problems so they could be solved. Investigative reporters today are no different.

• Exercise •

Have students find examples of depth and investigative stories and take the stories apart and analyze how they were organized and written. Identify the sources and possible problems getting the information.

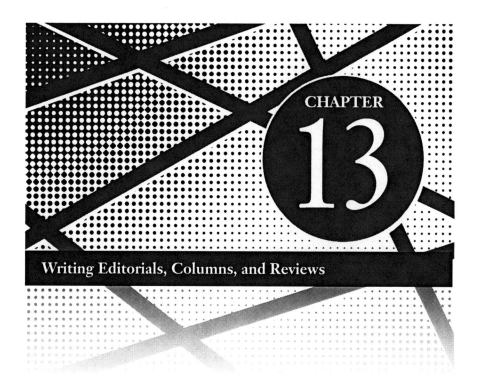

• The Purpose of Opinion Writing •

Trained journalists are taught to keep their opinion out of objective, factual news stories. Unfortunately, as we've learned already, the trend on air and in print today is to report fact and opinion together — a trend that's undermining the credibility of journalists everywhere.

This is not to say, however, that opinion writing has no place in journalism or public discourse. In fact, it has played an important role in the development of the republic. Opinion writing was instrumental in igniting the War of Independence. Radical leader Sam Adams' words helped define the goals of the Revolution, and Thomas Paine's *Common Sense* helped garner support for independence at a time when the struggle was in peril. His *Crisis* paper still rallies people in the cause for freedom today, proving that words do indeed matter:

> *These are the times that try men's souls. The summer soldier and the sunshine patriot will, in this crisis, shrink from the service of his*

country; but he that stands it NOW, deserves the love and thanks of man and woman. Tyranny, like hell, is not easily conquered; yet we have this consolation with us, that the harder the conflict the more glorious the triumph. What we obtain too cheap, we esteem too lightly — Tis dearness only that gives every thing its value. Heaven knows how to put a proper price upon its goods; and it would be strange indeed if so celestial an article as FREEDOM should not be highly rated.

The editorial function of the Press following the Revolution was no less important. A series of 85 articles were published throughout the country arguing for a new constitution. Referred to today as *The Federalist Papers,* the editorial campaign was among the most important journalistic enterprises in American history in that it rallied support for the new Constitution, a document that serves us still.

It's important, though, that journalists and citizens alike understand that the purpose of opinion writing is different from straight news. News gives us facts; opinion gives us an interpretation of facts, or some idea of truth. Although opinions should be based on facts, it is the job of the opinion writer to go beyond the facts to provide perspective and analysis or to persuade and promote or criticize. Sometimes opinion writing is there to fill in around the cold, hard facts to help us understand the gray areas of a story. Journalists can often give us insight into stories through their personal analysis that the facts alone can't reveal. This is especially true if the reporter has been covering a topic or area for a long time. His experience over the long term can help us understand the big picture.

Of course, it is always important to understand whose opinion you're getting. Is it someone you trust; is it someone who is intelligent enough to know a fact from an opinion? Are they in a position to really know more than you, or are they just blowing steam? Many of today's opinion writers have nothing to recommend them except the volume of their voice. Such blowhards can actually make it more difficult for us to learn the truth since their anger usually provides more heat than light and pollutes our reason with passion.

Nevertheless, for the journalist the point is not to avoid the use of commentary completely, but to segregate it so the reader knows that when he's reading a news story he's getting straight fact in context, and when he's reading an opinion piece he's getting a mixture of fact and opinion through the eyes of the commentator. In American journalism, therefore, it's important that all opinion pieces be labeled. Without such direction the reader assumes he is getting straight news when, in fact, he may not be getting that at all.

Labels might include *analysis*, which means the reporter is adding his perspective to help the reader understand the story better. *Letters to the editor* are comments from readers, and *opinions* are usually one-time articles written by those who hold a position of authority and have insight into a particular area. Although blogs could technically be written as straight news stories, they are usually synonymous with columns where the reporter is giving his own opinion along with the factual information. But in whatever form opinion comes, it is important that people see it for what it is.

In addition to analysis pieces, journalists need to understand how to write three kinds of opinion articles, including editorials, columns, and reviews.

• Writing the Editorial •

Editorials are opinion pieces that reveal the newspaper's journalistic or corporate position on a particular subject and carry the weight and authority of the newspaper or broadcast station. They often serve to explain the news, offer background information and historical perspective, predict where events are likely to go, and pass moral judgment on some issue. They explain, persuade, and evaluate. Although editorials may not change people's minds, they do often make them think. Editorials provide guidance and force the reader to reevaluate their own position as well as those of others about a particular subject. As such, they are often starting points for community and national debate.

Novice reporters aren't assigned to write editorials. The wisest and usually oldest journalists on the staff, people who are widely read and experienced, are given the task. At a small newspaper or broadcast station, the editor or owner may write them. At larger news outlets, an editorial board is responsible for writing them.

The editorial board answers directly to the editor in chief. It often includes six or seven journalists; some include a member of the community. The editorial page editor is in charge of deciding what subjects will be covered and which editorials will be written and by whom. The editorial page editor also is responsible for laying out the page.

Typically, the editorial writers will meet and discuss issues that are likely to concern, or should concern, their readers. The topics may be local, national, or international. The writers research the various agreed upon subjects and then write editorials supporting different and sometimes contradictory positions on each one. The editorial that makes the most sense and is most defensible is chosen. At other publications or broadcast stations, the angle of the editorial may be based upon the medium's political stance. Some newspapers are conservative; others are liberal, and their positions on a topic will reflect that.

At the beginning of the republic, many newspapers were known for a particular political slant and reported the news accordingly. As publishers found they could make more money by being objective and attracting more readers from both parties, news and commentary began to be segregated and more objective reporting was pursued. By the end of the nineteenth century, a separate editorial page reserved for opinion was well established.

Today, in addition, an opinion page often faces the editorial page. The opinion page, called the *op-ed* page, contains columns from columnists and opinion pieces from experts or authorities from government agencies, universities, or other areas.

Most editorial pages will include about four or five editorials stacked in a column under the heading *editorials*. An editorial cartoon may also be on the page along with the masthead — the box that includes a listing of the paper's principal editors. Also on the page, usually below the cartoon and next to the editorials and under the heading *letters*, will be a number of letters to the editor written by readers commenting on the news. Arguably, before the age of the Internet, this was the most important part of any newspaper, for this is where the community came to share their thoughts on the issues of the day. This was the corner tavern in 1776. It's where the democracy came to work.

Regardless of the subject, editorials are written to make a point, the point of the writer, and therefore are written to persuade the reader or listener to accept the writer's position. All effective persuaders understand their audience. Are they sympathetic, skeptical, hostile? Are they from the South, the North? Are they religious, gun owners, Democrats, Republicans, college educated? Every successful trial lawyer knows that winning and losing the case can occur during jury selection. Put another way, there's an old legal adage that says "a good lawyer knows the law, but a great lawyer knows the judge." Effective editorial writers understand that they must connect with their audience, and to do that they must understand their listener's values, experiences, and attitudes. What will motivate them? All of us bring bias to the table, and we look for the facts we agree with and often ignore the ones we don't agree with. Those who work to persuade others learn how to use that.

To be effective, the editorial writer must understand the various techniques that can be used to sway audiences. The foundation of all persuasion is built upon three elements: **pathos, ethos,** and **logos.** Most editorials use a combination of all three, but the mix depends upon the audience.

Pathos refers to what persuades us emotionally. We agree with the writer because something he said makes us feel good. We accept the writer's position on some gut level. Nearly all of modern advertising uses emotional persuasion because it's easier to appeal to our emotions than to make the case logically. We may not need the new car (logically) but we want the car (emotionally). Put a beautiful woman in the seat and it seals the deal. As we noted early in the text, we use our intellect and senses to decide the truth.

But emotions tend to trump reason. No one has to teach you how to feel, but it takes years of school to learn how to think logically. Writers can rely more heavily on pathos when the audience already is sympathetic to their position.

Ethos has to do with credibility and trust. Integrity, intellect, knowledge, commitment, sacrifice are all characteristics we admire, and we tend to trust and believe those who have them. Those diplomas on the wall at the doctor's office aren't there for decoration. They help persuade the patient that the doctor knows what he's talking about. Ethos is relied upon when the audience is wavering in its support. The patient is not sure he trusts the doctor completely. Seeing the diplomas helps ease his skepticism.

If pathos and ethos have to do with persuasion, **logos** has to do with logic, the prime ingredient in another persuasive technique — argumentation. Most editorials combine both persuasive and argumentative techniques. Logos is primarily used when the writer or speaker is facing a hostile audience. The arguer is trying to separate them from their emotions and force them to use their intellect.

Unfortunately, we often think of an argument as a heated exchange between people, something that separates them, but the real purpose of effective argument is to bring people together. It is a way to evaluate and test the different positions of the debaters and find which positions are best supported by the evidence and which are not. They also help us find where we agree and disagree so we can better figure out where we can compromise. And they help us find out what is true and what is not as we evaluate facts and positions logically.

It matters then how both the writer and reader approach an argument. Far too often we see people yelling at one another — or just yelling — and think this is normal. It isn't. If argument is to be effective, both sides must approach it with the attitude of exploring the truth, and with respect for the other side and with the process of debate itself. By bringing out contrary positions and the facts to support them, we force an evaluation of all aspects of the issue so we can see it more clearly.

This is not to be confused with what we see on talk radio, which usually offers only demagoguery and is not argumentation. In argument we look for reason, not passion, and we back it with evidence. Therefore, before we begin to talk about the role of argumentation in effective opinion writing—especially in editorials — we must first approach it with the right attitude. The goal is not hostility, but understanding, and our attitudes should reflect that.

Three kinds of reasoning are used in argumentation: **inductive, deductive,** and **Toulmin.** Reasoning is a method to reach a conclusion, judgment, or inference from facts. In Western Enlightenment thought, we rely heavily on reasoning. The Scientific Method, which came out of the Enlightenment, begins with a hypothesis that is proven or disproven with facts through investigation and experimentation.

Inductive reasoning begins with specific facts from which we draw a conclusion. When I go to the doctor and say I have a temperature, a headache, a stuffy nose, and a sister with a cold, the doctor makes a judgment on the basis of those facts and announces that I probably have a cold. The jump to this conclusion is called the *inductive leap.* Inductive reasoning can be faulty if the judgment is made from too few facts or facts that are not representative of the situation about which we are trying to draw a conclusion. That's why the doctor says I "probably" have a cold. These could be symptoms of something else. Consequently, the prudent physician would most likely order more tests or collect more evidence to make sure his diagnosis is correct.

Deductive reasoning has a different structure, a three-step process called a *syllogism*. It starts with a generalization that is widely accepted, called a *major premise*, that is then applied to a specific case that leads to a conclusion. For example:

> Major premise: *Large cars are safer than small cars in an accident.*
> Minor premise: *The Hummer is a large car.*
> Conclusion: *In an accident, it would be safer to be in a Hummer than in a small car.*

Based on the conclusion, the writer may take the reader to the next logical step and suggest he take action and buy a Hummer if he wants to be safe on the road.

Deductive reasoning can be faulty as well if you make a hasty or sweeping generalization as your major premise or if you accept a faulty minor premise or conclusion. For example:

> Major premise: *Thunderstorms kill people.*
> Minor premise: *A thunderstorm is coming.*
> Conclusion: *People will die.*

The major premise is sweeping because it lumps all thunderstorms, those that kill and those that don't, into one category. Since the major premise is not universally true, the logic fails. You would need to qualify the statement to fix the problem.

> Major premise: *Some thunderstorms have killed people.*
> Minor premise: *A thunderstorm is coming.*
> Conclusion: *It's possible that people will die.*

If your minor premise reverses the "if...then" relationship, the logic can also fail. For example:

> Major premise: *Students caught cheating must see the dean.*
> Minor premise: *Joe Green is going to see the dean.*
> Conclusion: *Joe Green must have been cheating.*

If students cheat they must see the dean, but the reverse isn't necessarily true — that students who see the dean must have cheated. There may be other reasons for seeing the dean.

Toulmin logic offers a different model. It uses a **claim** or proposition one is trying to prove, **data** or evidence, and the **warrant** — the explanation or reason that justifies and supports moving from the evidence to the claim. For example:

> Claim: *Airline pilots should be tested for drugs.*
> Data: *Several airline crashes have involved pilots on drugs.*
> Warrant: *People entrusted with public safety should not be allowed to fly while under the influence of drugs.*

If your warrant, or reasoning, is widely accepted, your audience will more likely accept your argument, particularly if it is supported by strong evidence.

Logic is a tool to help us find truth, but as noted, it can fail if not constructed properly. Other **logical fallacies** can get in the way as well. Work to avoid them in your own arguments and try to spot them in your opponents. These are but a few:

Ad hominem – Using personal attacks against the person instead of his argument. *Joe is a jerk.* He may be, but that has nothing to do with the logic of his argument.

Post hoc – Just because one event preceded another doesn't mean there is a cause and effect relationship. *Immigration is increasing and so is crime. Therefore, the immigrants must be causing the crime.* There may be other reasons for the increase.

Non sequitur — A conclusion is reached without any logical connection to the evidence. *Lots of people have cars, so there's no need for public transportation.* What about people who don't have cars, as well as problems with smog and congestion?

False analogy — Just because two things share some characteristics doesn't mean they share all. *If I can smoke a cigarette while I drive, I should be able to smoke marijuana while I drive.* But smoking marijuana impairs judgment and coordination while cigarettes do not.

Red herring — One side deflects attention away from the real issue by introducing some other issue. Suppose one side argues that a city needs stronger leash laws because several people in the Hispanic section have been attacked by stray dogs, to which the other side says: *Lots of those people are illegal aliens, so they have no right to protection.* The issue isn't immigration; it's public safety.

Begging the question — The arguer fails to offer proof for a debatable point. He assumes you will accept a premise that is controversial. *Guns cannot be regulated because that would violate the U.S. Constitution.* If that reason is true, you must prove it.

Appeals to faulty authority — Avoid phrases such as *experts say* and *studies show* because they fail to establish credibility. We are suspicious of them. Which experts? Hence, they weaken your argument.

Either/or fallacy — This assumes that a viewpoint can have only one of two opposite outcomes. *If the government stops funding public broadcasting, Big Bird will die.* This ignores the fact that funding also comes from donations and endowments and other sources which may be able to continue supporting Big Bird.

Half-truths — This is the stuff of political debates. One side takes something that is partially true and passes it off as completely true. *My opponent caused the financial crisis.* It is unlikely that any one leader has that much power. It is disingenuous and should raise a skeptical eyebrow. More often than not such a statement is only partly true, and in fact, other politicians on the other side may have had a hand in creating the problem. Your opponent is likely to catch such weak evidence and use it against you.

The Journalist's Primer

All argumentation assumes there are conflicting viewpoints and begins with an assertion or proposition — a viewpoint in the argument — that the writer endeavors to prove. This is called the *thesis*. Sometimes the thesis appears at the end of the paper, but if you start with the thesis, the reader understands your position immediately and is better able to evaluate your evidence and the reasoning that connects it to your proposition.

Remember to do research first to find your opinion, rather than start with an opinion based on ignorance and then find a few facts to support it.

The thesis is not a statement of fact. Facts are not controversial. We don't have to argue the existence of water. Facts are proven. For example, to say guns can kill is not in debate. But to connect that to a debatable viewpoint about guns — that imposing a longer waiting period to buy a firearm will reduce gun violence — is arguable.

The thesis also should be narrow and specific. The broader it is, the more difficult it is to prove. For example, to say current gun laws are insufficient to curb violence would require you to research and prove every gun law is faulty, an insurmountable task. It would be better to argue that a specific law isn't doing what it was designed to do in curbing gun violence.

Finally, the thesis usually will go further and call for some action, such as, *In an effort to curb violence, the federal government should increase the waiting period to buy guns.* The arguer would then have show a cause and effect relationship between increasing the waiting period and reducing violence.

It is equally important that you clarify the controversy at the beginning of the editorial and provide the reader with enough background information so he can understand the facts and issues behind the debate. This background information may come at the very beginning of the editorial or right after the writer has stated his thesis.

Background information is equally valuable to the writer. It helps him understand the roots of the debate and clarify the different positions in his mind. It's not enough that the debater understand his own argument; he must understand his opponent's position and the evidence supporting it as well, so he can argue effectively against it.

At the heart of the debate is evidence, the stuff that makes us accept the reasoning of the writer. Evidence should be specific, accurate, representative, unified, adequate, and dramatic. It may include personal observations and experiences, but because those are individual and not necessarily universal, it's often better to use facts and expert authority. All evidence should be tested for accuracy. Just because people agree with you doesn't make them good sources. They may have biases. In all cases, document your sources. It adds credibility or ethos to your editorial.

Organize your evidence to create the strongest possible effect, in general, ending with the most compelling point that emphasizes your proposition's validity. Effective organization will also help you better rebut your opponent's position. Finding some common ground or belief with your opponent from which to launch your own argument may make it more difficult for him to rebut your position.

The most effective writer also will acknowledge conflicting viewpoints and evidence before his opponent can bring them up. This technique undercuts your opponent's argument and allows you to handle it to your advantage. If your opponent's position has some merit, say so, then go on to show how it's also flawed. You will appear more knowledgeable and reasonable since you are willing to see the merit in contrary opinions. Such action makes your audience more receptive to your position. Remember, you're trying to convince, not alienate. This technique further helps you find flaws in your own argument as well as in your opponent's.

The structure of the editorial can take on many forms. It can be narrative, a technique in which you tell a story with a point. It can start with description to set an emotional scene. It can take the form of a formal debate. Which technique you use should come after you have explored several options and selected the one that will present your position in the strongest light.

To understand how the various parts fit together, it's useful to start with the simplest structure. This also gives a clear idea of what an argument looks like on paper. By reducing your editorial to one-sentence components, you can distill your argument to its essence before expanding it more fully. Note the following mini editorial:

1. **Thesis** — *College students who want to learn to write effective editorials should practice writing them in class, not just at home.*
2. **Background** — *Traditional lecture teaching methods are coming under attack from higher education officials for lack of effectiveness.*
3. **Argument** — *Students have learned to write more logically working in class under the watchful eye of their teachers.*
4. **Evidence** — *A U.S. Department of Education study revealed student papers written in class received 30 percent higher grades in logical construction than those written at home.*
5. **Counter-argument** — *Homework gives students more time to ponder their assignments.*
6. **Evidence** — *Most people who construct arguments — lawyers — work on them for days at home.*
7. **Rebuttal** — *Students can't argue as well as trained lawyers.*
8. **Evidence** — *Lawyers spend a minimum of three years in law school learning to write arguments.*
9. **Conclusion** — *College students who practice writing their editorials in class produce better work.*
10. **Call to action** — *Professors should provide students with in-class practice time to write editorials.*

Reason carefully as you write or evaluate arguments. Is the purpose of the writer and the editorial clear? Has the issue been stated clearly? Is there enough background information to help the reader understand the issue? Is there adequate, accurate, and relevant evidence, and does it support the writer's arguments? Is the writer assuming when he should not? Have the counter-arguments been addressed? Are there logical fallacies? Does the attitude of the writer encourage understanding or hostility?

Editorial writers should remember that their job is to provide honest, effective guidance to their audience. To this end they should meet certain standards.

First, they should endeavor to be wise and broadly educated. They must be honest. They must realize they carry the burden of public trust, and their job is one of service. Personal gain or interest should never be at the heart of their work. If they are to gain the public's respect, they must hold themselves to the highest standards. Half-truths and that which tends to mislead or distort should be avoided. People should never be placed in a false light.

Editorial writers must realize they are also in the reporting business and their editorials should be based on solid facts in context. Arguments should be clear and conclusions should be based on the facts. Public discourse is at the heart of any democracy. And those who disagree with the editorial writer's position should be given time and space to voice their contrary positions. If new information comes to light that refutes the editorial, the writer should correct it, updating his position and changing the conclusion when necessary.

• Writing the Column •

If the editorial is the voice of the newspaper, the column is the voice of the writer. As with any opinion piece, it must be labeled or presented as such since it reflects the personal view of the author. Unlike straight news stories, columns are often boxed with a clever title and the picture of the writer or they may be placed on an opinion page or on a page that deals with the subject of the column.

They may be on any subject, though most columnists write on a particular topic such as politics or sports or any area of interest that is likely to attract an audience. They may be personal and deal with nostalgia or humor. Or they may be on very specific areas of interest such as horoscopes or advice to the lovelorn. Religion, technology, health, law, gardening, personal finance, and personal fitness are a few of the more popular ones. Successful columnists usually offer a unique writing style or perspective that attracts readers. They add personality and a human touch to news outlets that usually offer mostly problems and pain.

Good columnists are good reporters first. Their columns must contain new information. Columnists who spend their time pontificating on things others already know eventually go unread. Columnists are most often feature writers with an attitude. They can be funny, analytical, sarcastic, but they all present a unique perspective. They are not objective; they're not trying to be.

Although beginning reporters think it looks like fun, column writing can be daunting. To come up with a clever subject two or three or even five times a week is difficult since it involves more than just going out and finding news and reporting it. The columnist must go beyond the news; he must add perspective to it, which makes the task doubly difficult.

• Writing the Review •

Those who wish to become critics should first become experts in the subject they intend to critique. Like columns, reviews involve more than just the writer jabbering on about what he likes or doesn't like, though many who call themselves reviewers do just that.

The review endeavors to pass judgment on some artistic enterprise by breaking it into its component parts and analyzing why each does or does not work. It could be a book, a play, a movie, a painting, a concert, an architectural design, or any other creative endeavor. And to do that well, the reviewer needs to be an expert in the area he critiques.

The purpose of the review is to educate the reader about the strengths and weaknesses of the artistic work. A review gives the artist an appraisal of his work from someone knowledgeable in his own field, and it gives the audience insight into why the work has succeeded or failed and why the reader should or should not read it, hear it, or go see it.

Reviews help promote culture. They bring the world of art to the attention of the community, encouraging discussion and creating an atmosphere for participation. They promote the business of art and introduce the next generation to creative expression. Reviews help us understand our government, our lives, and our world. Business and science — that's how we live. Art helps show us why we live. Reviews help us understand that.

For those who want to grow up to be reviewers, the goal should first be to learn the craft or profession they wish to critique. They should themselves be authors, painters, musicians and others who spend their lives in the world of art. Such knowledge also provides credibility to the review. We are more inclined to respect and believe those who have done it themselves. Even the sports commentators we see on television were themselves at one time star players. That's why they were hired to explain and pass judgment on the work of other players. The best teachers didn't just read it out of a book. They did it first.

• Exercise •

Identify various columns, reviews, and editorials in a newspaper. Discuss their differences.

Then critique an editorial from *The New York Times* or some other daily newspaper, identifying the thesis, the background information, the arguments and evidence, the counter arguments and evidence, the rebuttal and evidence, the conclusion and the call to action. Note the type of logic used and whether the writer used pathos, ethos, or logos or a mix of the three. Are there any logical fallacies? Is the structure narration, description, or some other form? Is the editorial convincing, given its probable audience?

Have the students identify a position in a controversy they feel passionate about and then write a mini editorial supporting the side with which they disagree. Critique.

• Organization •

To fully understand the editorial process, journalists must understand how it fits in with the overall newspaper organization. The modern newspaper has five departments, all of which are controlled by the publisher. The departments include advertising, editorial, production, circulation, and business.

The advertising department is responsible for selling and designing display and classified advertising. Display ads include the big retail ads that display what is being sold. Classified ads are those two or three-line ads individuals place in a section near the back. Newspapers make most of their money from advertising, less from subscription and street sales. Both are important — not just for sellers and buyers and readers — but for the democracy. First, the amount of ads sold determines the size of the newspaper. The more ads that are sold, the more pages can be published. Also, if the democracy is to work, everyone — even the poorest — must have access to information. By using advertising to pay for most of the costs of the newspaper, subscription costs can be kept low, enabling even poor people to afford information. And by including both display and classified advertising, even poor people can participate economically since they also can afford to buy a little ad at the back of the newspaper. True, the ad is small, but it's in the same number of newspapers as the big display ads, which means that technically just as many shoppers can see it.

It is also for this reason that news organizations don't pay for news. It is counter productive to maintaining the democracy. Paying for news adds to the cost of news and makes it more difficult for the poorest in society to be informed and participate in the democratic process. Technically, therefore, when you buy a newspaper you are paying for the gathering, writing, packaging, and distributing of news. The news itself is public domain, that is, it's free to anyone who bothers to go out and collect it. Remember that before the development of the printing press, the Enlightenment, and the American democracy, information was available only to those who could afford it, resulting in a two-tiered society of educated and uneducated people that made it difficult for the poor to rise above their station. The American press and its goal of disseminating information cheaply ensures that doesn't happen, and that task rests with the editorial department.

The editorial department is responsible for gathering and writing the news. This is where the reporters and editors work. After the advertising department sells and lays out the ads, the whole process moves to the editorial department where the editors decide what news to put in the space that's left over after the ads have been inserted. This is called the *news hole*.

From there the process moves to the production department. Production is responsible for printing the paper. They are responsible for making the plates and running the presses. The quality of the printing job is dependent upon their skill.

Once the newspaper is printed it's time for the circulation department to distribute the newspaper. Workers here include everyone from the paperboy on the street corner to the trucker who carries the paper to distant cities to the person who places it in the vending machines at the courthouse.

Finally, the business office is responsible for billing and accounting and all the other tasks that are required to run a business. These include accountants and business managers, promotional people and, in some cases, personnel managers.

It is important to understand that editors and writers are part of a team effort to publish the day's news. And even though the news is at the heart of what a newspaper is all about, it could not exist without the other parts.

Although the publisher is responsible for running the overall newspaper, it is the editor in chief who is responsible for the editorial department. The editor decides policy and is largely the figurehead of the entire newspaper. Ultimately, what does and does not get published is up to him.

The managing editor is under him. He is responsible for the day-to-day coordination of the newsroom, including the various editors as well as the reporters and photographers who work under them. Each editor is responsible, in turn, for a different area of news. The city editor is responsible for all the news in the metropolitan area. The state editor oversees the gathering of news outside the metro area but within the state. Sports editors are responsible for sports; feature editors are responsible for features; business editors are responsible for business news; photo editors are responsible for the photos and photographers; and national editors are responsible for news from around the nation, etc.

The managing editor is also responsible for the news editor, who, in turn, is responsible for the copyeditors and copy desk where most of the editing takes place. The news editor is largely responsible for supervision of copyediting, writing headlines, and designing page makeup. He gets the stories after the other editors have finished editing their reporters' work.

In the final analysis, putting out a newspaper is rather like conducting an orchestra. Everyone has a different part to play and every part is important.

• Purpose •

It's said that stories are not written; they are rewritten. Writing is a process of lining up thoughts and facts in some kind of coherent order so the reader sees and understands what the writer sees and understands. The idea is to transfer a thought from one mind to another as completely and accurately as possible.

And that takes work and lots of revision because no one writes perfect prose the first time through.

Faulty writing can be the result of faulty thinking, of not really understanding what we're trying to say because we haven't thought about it long enough or clearly enough. Or it can result from not fully understanding the rules of grammar or punctuation. Sometimes, it's lazy writing, of not working hard enough to say things simply or with the right words. Writing too quickly may get more words on paper but it leaves less time for thought and reflection. Ironically, the more words one uses, the greater the chance for misunderstanding. The best writing is always clean and lean — and simple.

Editing endeavors to step in and clean up the writer's thought process as well as his words. It is, in a sense, a matter of quality control — making sure that we are saying what we think we are saying and saying it as best we can. Writers often forget that they may be too close to the story. They then make the mistake of thinking the reader knows what they know. As a result they don't always explain things fully. Editors put themselves in the place of the reader. They aren't familiar with the story either; therefore, if they don't understand it, neither will the reader.

• Procedure •

Writing, then, is a two-step process. First we write and then we edit. Although this sounds obviously simple, many writers make the mistake of trying to do both at once and without the benefit of an editor — often with disastrous effects. Of course, careful writers will always review, revise, and edit their own work, but the eyes of another person catch mistakes the author overlooks. Effective editing can make a dull story shine, catch mistakes that can muddy understanding and protect the writer and publication from legal trouble. The job of the editor is to make writers better. And all good writers have editors.

One of the dangers of the web is the speed with which new information can be distributed blindly. The temptation is to shortchange the editing process or skip it altogether to get the information out quickly. This leads to mistakes and the distribution of false or misleading information. The advent of new technology has made editors more important than ever. Ironically, shrinking newsroom profits have eliminated many of them. Bloggers have an even more difficult time since they often work on their own without the benefit of an editor.

The best editors will ask the reporter one question after he comes in from his assignment to write the story. What is your story about? As simple as it sounds, it is often difficult to answer because the writer hasn't synthesized his notes enough to figure out the essence of his story. Therefore, before the writer sits down to write, he must be able to state in one simple sentence — My story is about ... This clarifies his mission in his mind and gives his writing direction.

The next step comes once the writer has finished the story and before he gives it to the editor. He must strike an attitude, become cynical and mean with the story, and try to make fun of it. He must ask himself, what the hell is wrong with this, who would write that sentence that way, what has been left out of this, how can I make this better? He must do that with each word, each sentence, each paragraph as well as the overall structure.

The best writers are always their own worst critics. If you want to be good, you must be brutal — with everything. The only way to get to the point where you can do that is to read good writing so you can compare and contrast it to bad writing. Then when you write something, you can tell just how good or bad your writing is in comparison. The more you do that, the more your writing will improve. Your editing skills will improve as well.

Good writers go through their work at least twice, editing and revising again and again. The first time they look for big problems with the story — missing information and problems with context. They ask themselves if they have answered who, what, when, where, how, and why. Does the lead reflect the real story? Is the body in the inverted pyramid? Have they identified their sources and attributed all the information? The writer is looking at the big picture. He is asking himself if he has truly identified the story and revealed it well.

The next time through writers look at the details — the grammar, spelling, punctuation, word choice, etc. They check to make sure they are following proper style guidelines.

The Journalist's Primer

Style in this case isn't how a particular writer writes, but the usage standards demanded of journalists working for a specific medium. These are standards that go beyond the basic rules of English. For example, print journalists write 10 a.m., not 10:00 AM. These standards give uniformity and familiarity to news story style. The rules are codified in style manuals, which all journalists are taught in school. Most follow *The Associated Press Style Manual*. But some newspapers, like *The New York Times*, have their own style rules. Broadcast rules differ from print rules. Effective reporting courses always include style instruction using the appropriate style guide.

Finally, writers try to say things as simply and clearly as possible and with the fewest words necessary to do so. The goal is clear, concise, complete, compelling writing. Is it easy to read and understand the first time through? If you have to reread a sentence to understand it, it's too complicated or fuzzy.

Although most editing is done on a computer screen, sometimes it's helpful to edit with copyediting marks after printing the story out on paper. By seeing and labeling all the mistakes before you correct them, it's often easier to see if you are committing a pattern of errors. All writers must memorize and understand the common copyediting commands and symbols. You never know when an editor is going to use them or expect you to use them.

Once the writer finishes the story, it passes to the editor, who will repeat the same process, but more objectively. The problem with writers is that they are in love with their words. Editors aren't afflicted with such love affairs. They are brutal, uncaring, unfeeling people — at least from the perspective of writers. Editors will review the internal logic or structure of a story. Do the elements naturally and logically connect? They cut words and rewrite sentences and rearrange paragraphs, trying to make the words say the most they can in as little space as possible.

In addition to looking for the common mistakes already mentioned, editors also challenge the accuracy of the story. They question facts and sources. And they play gatekeeper. Is the story right for the audience? That is, does it speak to something the reader needs or wants to know? What is the news value of the story? Why is the story being presented? They want to know why it's important, to whom it's important, and how it will affect the recipient.

They also will look for commentary in the story. What words has the writer used? Are they color words? Are they prejudicial? Has the writer been fair? It's not the job of the writer to tell people what they want to hear. This isn't public relations. Tell the facts, all the facts necessary to understand the story, whether it's unflattering or not. Editors help keep reporters honest with their reporting. Sometimes writers are tempted to pull punches, to not be as brutally honest as they need to be. The editor's job is to make sure they tell the story true.

Broadcast journalists need to edit their on-air delivery as well as their copy. An inflection here and a raised eyebrow there can add commentary to a story as easily as a misused word.

Editors also will check to make sure controversial statements are attributed and verified. Journalists should never allow exaggerated claims or questionable statements to go unchallenged.

Stories should be updated as new information becomes available, and new information may reveal that earlier stories were inaccurate. It is the job of the journalist to always give the reader the best obtainable version of the truth. As the story unfolds, the reader needs to be brought up to date. Good editors tend to remember what's been covered and will challenge the reporter to revisit stories for new developments.

Editors also try to improve copy by looking for clichés, stock phrases, and other story padding. Sometimes it's a matter of tightening the writing: *in spite of* becomes *despite*. They will look for ways to explain things more clearly. Sometimes they will suggest the writer use an example or description. They will change wording from passive to active voice, prefer concrete words to those that are abstract. Writers also should avoid slang and foreign words.

Writers need to be mindful of a word's connotation. *Regime* carries a more negative meaning than *government*. But don't fall into the trap of using politically correct speech or euphemisms either. People don't *pass away*; they *die*. Call things what they are.

• Other Editing Tasks •

Editors are responsible for more than editing copy. They write headlines, watch out for legal problems such as libel and invasion of privacy, design pages, preside over news budget meetings, select what news is disseminated, and, as noted earlier, manage the editorial department.

Headlines carry the gist of a story in a few words. In today's Internet world where search engines categorize stories by key words in the lead, editors must make sure the right words are up front to summarize the story correctly. Strong nouns and verbs are essential.

Editors also make sure legalese and other technical language is translated so the reader understands what is being said. It is essential that it be translated accurately. Technical language has very specific meaning. *Malice* does not mean *ill will* when it comes to legal language. Remember, close isn't good enough. The translation must be precise.

Editors understand also that stories are communicated by more than just words. Page design, typography, graphs, charts, photos — all of these help communicate. Readers do judge a book by its cover, and they will also judge your story by how it's laid out on the page. The bigger the display is, the more important the story and vice versa.

Organizing elements on the page is part of the world of graphic design. It refers to the total design, arrangement, and appearance of printed matter — whether on newsprint or a computer screen. And in today's online world, it's vital that all journalists — writers and editors alike — be proficient graphic designers. A poor visual presentation can ruin even the best story.

Editors begin the process of design by sketching out where the different elements go on a *dummy*, a sheet of paper or online template that gives a rough idea of what the page will look like when finished. Designers understand that to be effective everything must be legible and logical. Editors must be concerned with balance, contrast, and proportion, essential in today's Internet world with the use of boxes, news summaries, photos, charts, and bulleted lists. Scattering them across the page won't work.

They also understand that in Western culture, the eye moves from left to right and top to bottom on the page. People recognize words by their shapes, not by their individual letters. And the task of reading becomes even easier if the reader can take in a whole line of words at a glance. Because of the way the eye works, we also don't write in all caps or use script or cursive typeface. Flush left text that is justified is easier to read than flush right. Columns of print that are too long or too narrow are more difficult to read.

Serif typeface is generally easier for the eye to read for long blocks of body type than sans-serif typeface. Type, measured in points, should be easy to read — on newsprint this means 9 or 10 points. Black type is preferable. And stick with one or two styles of type. Too many are distracting. These are but a few of the rules of good design.

Generally, the simpler the design is, the better. This is especially true on a computer screen, which is smaller. Editors who tend to cram too much onto the screen make it difficult for the eye to know where to go.

Good design means related elements should be near one another. The headline should be near the story and the captions near their illustrations. What's not on the page matters as much as what is. The use of white space should help guide the reader's eyes. Additionally, every page should have a focal point, a place where the eye naturally goes, an entry point. One of the major problems with computer screen design is that all the elements are often the same size, confusing the eye about where to go first. One element should dominate the page to give the reader a place to begin. In the end, the page should be aesthetically pleasing, logical, and easy to read.

After the story has been edited, placed on the page and set in type, a *proof* of the page is printed, which is then edited again for typos and other mistakes. This is the last chance to correct things before the paper is printed. Editors make sure the headlines go with the right stories, that dates and numbers are correct, that pictures are not upside down, etc.

Editing is equally important for broadcasters, of course. While the quest for accuracy and context remains the same, electronic media have some differences. Where print copy is edited for the eye, broadcast copy is edited for the ear. Print is edited for length; broadcast is edited for time. Leads must be short and edited copy should be retyped. Broadcasters don't have time to translate editing marks while they're reading stories on air. Since most listeners aren't inclined to record broadcasts so they can go back and study them more fully later, broadcasters know that the audience must understand the story on the first read. As a result, some elements of the story are repeated.

Broadcast style is different from print style. For example, most abbreviations are eliminated, capitalization is used more freely and words that are emphasized are underlined. TV tells stories primarily with pictures. The words are important, but the audience expects good video to accompany them. Most broadcasters will try to end their newscast on a pleasant note with a feature story or brite. Maintaining pace is important. Alternating talent can help, moving from the anchor to reporter to tape.

A newscast is built from top to bottom. What comes first often determines the rest of the program. Hard news generally comes first in the broadcast. Radio usually leads with what's newest while TV goes with the biggest thing that's happened or the best video. Stories are grouped logically by topic. Police stories go with police stories, and so on. Television and radio broadcasts are prepared much the same way, but television is a more involved process because of the visuals. The juxtaposition of copy to video and newscast to commercial and how you get from one to the other requires planning. Direct cuts, picture fades, station titles, and the anchor saying "more news in a minute" are all devices that can be employed.

The time of day also matters as to how a show is edited. Morning programs review what happened while everyone was asleep. Midday shows keep listeners up to date. Early evening broadcasts inform us of what happened while we were at work. And late night programs recap the day.

The job of editing, regardless of the medium, is varied and demanding, rather like juggling eight balls at once while drinking a glass of water. But in the end, it's an important job. Editors are responsible for giving us the first draft of history.

• Exercise •

Give students a poorly written story and have them edit it using the proper copyediting commands. Then provide them with a horizontal and a vertical photo, five more stories, a box of bulleted information, and a graph, as well as audio and video. Have them write headlines for the stories and makeup and design a newspaper page. Then have them do the same thing for an online page. Finally, have them rewrite the print news story for broadcast, add the audio and video, and design a newscast.

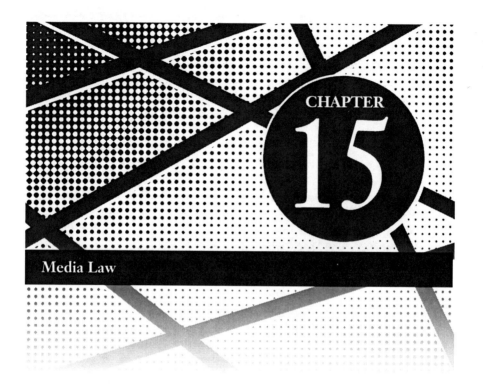

Media Law

• The First Amendment and Free Expression •

Congress shall make no law respecting an establishment of religion, or prohibiting the free exercise thereof; or abridging the freedom of speech, or of the press; or the right of the people peaceably to assemble, and to petition the Government for a redress of grievances.

– The First Amendment to the U.S. Constitution

Arguably, the mass media is the only private business protected in the U.S. Constitution. As we've learned already, there's a good reason for this. Without the robust interchange of ideas, the people cannot bring about the political and social changes they desire. From the beginning we have used the private press to distribute those ideas. To make sure that interchange remains unfettered and beyond the reach of those in power who would manipulate the media to their own political advantage, the founders had the good sense to protect the Press from the power of government.

It is important, therefore, that journalists understand this foremost law that protects them. It exists to protect each citizen's right to pursue his own idea of truth. It exists so we can know about our government and those who run it. And it exists as the foundation of U.S. media law.

• The Boundaries of Free Expression •

Although The First Amendment is written in absolute terms — Congress shall make *no* law — the U.S. Supreme Court has taken the position that there are indeed boundaries. For example, you can't yell *fire* in a crowded movie theater. You can't libel people with impunity. You can't use a sound truck in a residential neighborhood at 2 a.m. to announce your candidacy for office. You can't incite the imminent and likely overthrow of the government.

The U.S. Constitution provides citizens with more than just the right to free speech and press. It also gives the government the power to pass laws for the health, safety, and welfare of its citizens. What happens when these rights collide?

The court first wrestled with the question of just how much free speech is too much free speech in *Schenck v. U.S.* (249 U.S. 47) in 1919. A socialist named Charles Schenck passed out leaflets opposing U.S. involvement in World War I. Schenck and others were arrested and charged with violating the country's Espionage Act, which basically made it a crime to interfere with the war effort. The pamphlets urged young men to resist the draft.

Justice Oliver Wendell Holmes wrote the opinion for the court in rejecting Schenck's argument that the law violated his First Amendment rights:

> *The question in every case is whether the words used, are used in such circumstances and are of such a nature as to create a clear and present danger that they will bring about the substantive evils that Congress has a right to prevent. It is a question of proximity and degree.*

This *clear and present danger* test said Congress had a right to prevent conduct that might be harmful to the nation. But just what was *clear* and *present*? The court continued to struggle with the question until *Brandenburg v. Ohio* (395

U.S. 444) in 1969 when it refined its answer. In that case a leader of the Ku Klux Klan was convicted of violating an Ohio sedition law for suggesting that some revenge might need to be taken against the government for what it considered to be suppression of the white race. The court narrowed the Holmes test by noting that the law must distinguish between advocating ideas and inciting illegal conduct:

> *The constitutional guarantees of free speech and free press do not permit a state to forbid or proscribe advocacy of the use of force or of law violation except where such advocacy is directed to inciting or producing imminent lawless action and is likely to incite or produce such actions.*

The court thus answered the question of how much free speech is too much free speech by noting that you can talk about something all you want — up until the talk directed to incite or produce lawless action is *imminent* and *likely* to do just that. For legal scholars and jurists *imminent* and *likely* are more precise than *clear* and *present*. *Imminent* is right before it happens and *likely* is 51 percent. The facts of each case will determine just how imminent and likely such lawless action is. To say, therefore, that we should kick all the politicians out and start a new government is protected speech. Such speech is not imminent and likely to bring about the fall of the government. But to use words that are imminent and likely to cause others to get their guns and march on Washington would be going too far.

The Bill of Rights, which includes the First Amendment, contains many of the fundamental liberties that define us as a people and a nation. They are fundamental to what we are about and therefore represent our most important liberties. As a result, the Court gives them a preferred position when they bump up against other interests. On the other hand, when free press and fair trial — also guaranteed as a fundamental liberty — collide, the Court attempts to balance both rights.

The Court purposefully tilts the scales of justice in favor of free expression when that right is challenged against another non-fundamental right because all our other rights are dependent on free speech and press. This gives certainty and a degree of predictability to the law. Therefore, if the government attempts to censor someone because they don't like what or how they're saying it, the Court essentially says, "Okay, we'll listen to what you have to say Government, but you've got two strikes against you from the start because free expression is vital and we're not inclined to take it away."

To help the Court decide these cases, it uses two primary tests. They include *strict scrutiny* and *intermediate scrutiny*.

When the government is trying to take away free speech on the basis of content — that is, what you're trying to say — that constitutes censorship, the most egregious evil in a democracy, and the Court demands the government meet very strict standards before it will allow such action. This constitutes strict scrutiny. In such situations, the government must show that it has a compelling state interest, an interest that is so important that it goes to the safety of the country and therefore trumps the need for free expression. For example, we would not want to publish where our troop ships were during times of war. The ships would be sunk; we would lose the war; and the country would perish. But most of the time, the government loses censorship cases because trumping a fundamental liberty is difficult.

Intermediate scrutiny is used when the government is not trying to prevent you from saying something on the basis of content, but is trying to regulate when, where, and in what manner you say it. We call these time, place, and manner restrictions. In intermediate cases, the government must show a substantial state interest, something that's important but doesn't rise to the level of a compelling state interest.

For example, the government would be allowed to pass a law saying you could not use a sound truck in a residential neighborhood at 2 a.m. to announce that you were running for governor. The substantial state interest the government would argue is the peoples' right to sleep. The government would argue it's not trying to stop you from getting your message out; it's just saying you can't do it that way at that time. Since the Constitution gives the government the right to pass laws for the benefit of the health, safety, and welfare of its citizens, the Court would likely rule in its favor, provided the government did not prevent you from using alternate means to get your message out.

The Court will also look to where the speech occurred in helping it decide cases. Traditional public forums such as street corners, public parks, and the steps of city hall receive the most free speech protection. Historically, that's where people have come to speak. Designated public forums such as auditoriums and fairgrounds are often used for expression, but the government has more control over them because they are designated for a particular purpose. Public property that is not a public forum includes prisons and military bases and may be deemed off limits for expressive purposes. Finally, no free expression guarantees exist on someone else's private property.

• Libel •

Understanding the First Amendment and how it's applied is only the initial step for journalists. Just because the Constitution protects the Press does not mean that the Press is without constraints.

Laws against defamation historically have given journalists the most legal trouble and curtailed press power the most. Defamation is the publication or broadcast of a false statement that harms someone's reputation. A statement that lowers a person's esteem in the community, causes him to be shunned, hurts his business or professional reputation, or holds him up to contempt or ridicule is actionable. Words or pictures or drawings can all be libelous.

The law against defamation is a centuries-old law known as a tort, a civil wrong. Defamation falls under state law, except in media cases when constitutional law also must be considered because of the First Amendment. Defamation comes in two varieties: libel and slander. Libel is printed defamation. Slander is spoken defamation. Only those who have been libeled or slandered can sue and the right to sue dies with the individual. Of the two, libel is worse because it theoretically can do more harm. When one slanders another, the words dissipate in the air along with the potential to do more damage. But libel continues to harm each time someone reads or sees it. Despite this difference, defamation involving the mass media is generally always considered libel, even if it's spoken, because it's usually taped and because of the extensive reach of the media and the greater harm that can result from it.

Simple common law libel contains four elements that must be proven by the plaintiff in court:

Defamation — Defamation is a false statement that impeaches someone's honesty, integrity, virtue, sanity, etc. If the words themselves are defamatory — such as calling someone a murderer or rapist — then the statement is libelous on its face or *libel per se*. But libel can also occur if the defamation becomes apparent by adding extrinsic facts — *libel per quod*. For example, a newspaper mistakenly publishes a report that a professional golfer won a match on Saturday when the match really occurred on Friday. Saying someone won a golf match is not libelous, unless the winner is a devout member of a religion that believes Saturday is the Sabbath and is a day for meditation and rest, in which case the mistaken story suggests he is not devout to his religion.

Identification — The offensive language must be *of or concerning* the plaintiff. This means the person bringing the suit must prove that a reasonable reader, listener, or viewer would understand that the offending statement referred to him. This does not mean he has to be identified by name. If the plaintiff can show additional facts that would indicate the statement was about him, it would be enough. Generally, if the statement refers to members of a small group, each member must be able to show the statement was about him. The larger the group is, the more difficult that becomes.

Publication — The libelous statement must be communicated to a third person that understands it. This constitutes publication. Only the intent to publish is required. Saying you didn't intend to defame is no defense. Each time the libel is repeated is a separate publication and is actionable, except multiple copies of the same issue of a newspaper containing the libel are considered a single publication. All those with control over publishing the damaging statement can be held liable if they know or should know of the defamatory content. For example, this generally includes publishers, writers, and editors, but not necessarily pressmen and paperboys.

Damage — The defamation must have harmed the plaintiff's reputation. General damages are presumed and need not be proved in common law libel.

Common law libel is fairly straightforward. One person sues another in state court for damaging their reputation. But when the mass media becomes a defendant, things get sticky. That's because when the defamation involves a matter of public concern, which is just about anything the media publishes or broadcasts, there are First Amendment concerns. As a result, the plaintiff must prove two additional elements — **falsity** and **fault**.

The underlying reason for making it more difficult for the plaintiff to win a suit against the mass media is to protect the free flow of information on matters of public concern. This First Amendment concern was established in *New York Times Co. v. Sullivan* (376 U.S. 254) in 1964. In that case, the police commissioner of the Montgomery Police Department sued some civil rights advocates for libel after they ran an ad in the paper contending public officials had used illegal tactics to quell peaceful demonstrations. Although not mentioned by name in the ad, the police commissioner argued that the comments about the police reflected on him. The Alabama Supreme Court ruled in his favor, but the case was appealed to the U.S. Supreme Court, which overruled it.

Although there were factual errors in the ad, the Court ruled that unless the commissioner could prove that the paper published the ad knowing it was false or that it had serious doubts about its veracity when it published it, the paper wasn't liable. The Court called publishing known falsehoods or reckless disregard for the truth *actual malice*.

At common law, falsity was presumed. Now the claim that the libelous statement was indeed a false statement had to be proved by the plaintiff. Winning a libel suit against the media suddenly became much more difficult.

To make matters even muddier, the Court has ruled that the fault requirement changes depending on who the plaintiff is. Public officials and public figures must prove actual malice. A public official is someone who has control over public policy, safety, or finances. A public figure is one who has achieved fame or notoriety or who has assumed a central role in a controversy, which is a matter of public concern.

People who are not public officials or public figures are considered private individuals. Private people defamed in the media need prove only the four basic elements of common libel unless the defamatory statement involves a matter of public concern. In such cases the plaintiff must prove negligence of the media. Negligence is defined as failure to exercise reasonable care. The Court looks to content, form, and context of the statement to determine if something is a matter of public concern. In some situations, the Court has ruled a person may be a public person while at other times a private person depending upon the facts of the case.

Various defenses exist to libel. Libel is a false statement that defames. So proving the statement is factually true is an absolute defense to a charge of libel. Consent is also a defense. Those who consent to the publication of defamatory material generally cannot sue for libel.

Privilege is a legal concept that protects certain speech. Absolute privilege protects communication in legislative forums, courtrooms, and administrative and executive branches of government when it's part of the official function of government. For example, a witness in court cannot be sued for saying something bad about the defendant. Qualified privilege is granted to the media when it reports what happens in an official proceeding or an official report or statement. The protection exists even if the material defames someone. But unlike absolute privilege, which cannot be lost, qualified privilege, as the name notes, can be lost if the reporter fails to give a fair and accurate or truthful summary of the meeting or the report.

Free speech wouldn't mean much if we couldn't express our opinions. Consequently, opinion speech is also protected. Rhetorical hyperbole, an unbelievable, exaggerated statement, is one form of opinion that falls in this category. The Court has ruled that a reasonable person would not accept such statements as fact. The key is that it must be clear from the tone or content that the speech is exaggerated.

The Court can use one of two tests to determine if a statement should be regarded as fact or opinion. The first test has its roots in the First Amendment and looks at four things:

First, can the statement be proved true or false?

Second, What is the ordinary meaning of the words? Calling someone a turkey doesn't mean you really think they are a bird that gobbles.

Third, in what context did the journalist use the statement? We expect to find facts in a news story and opinions in an editorial.

Fourth, what is the social context of the statement? Did the remark occur in lecture by a scientist or was it at a political rally where we would be more inclined to hear opinion?

Fair comment defenses are also available. This second common law defense looks at three things:

First, again, can the statement be proved true or false?

Second, is the statement a matter of legitimate public concern?

Third, is there a factual basis for the opinion? It is always a good idea to note the facts that give rise to the opinion, and the facts on which you base your opinion must not be misstated.

Finally, retractions, an attempt to apologize and set the record straight after you have defamed someone, may mitigate the damage. More than half the states have some kind of retraction statute. Journalists should review the statutes in the state where they work.

One additional tort often associated with libel is worth mentioning. And that is **intentional infliction of emotional distress**. The courts look to see whether the defendant acted outrageously. To win such cases the plaintiff must show that the defendant's conduct was intentional or reckless, that it was extreme, and that it caused the plaintiff severe emotional distress.

• Invasion of Privacy •

Invasion of privacy, like libel, is a tort, but a more recent law. Like libel, only people who have had their privacy invaded can sue, and the right to sue dies with the individual and cannot be assigned to another. Population growth and concentration and technological developments have contributed to an increase in privacy lawsuits. Simply put, it's easier to invade someone's space today.

Invasion of privacy is a violation of a person's right to be let alone. Although not specifically mentioned in the U.S. Constitution, the Court has ruled that the right to privacy is implicit in the Bill of Rights. Freedom of association in the First Amendment, limits on the government's power to quarter soldiers in private homes in the Third Amendment, protection from unreasonable search and seizure in the Fourth Amendment, and bans against self-incrimination in the Fifth Amendment all imply a right to privacy.

Furthermore, the underlying social and legal philosophies on which the country is founded — that the pursuit of truth, life, liberty, property, self-fulfillment is an individual endeavor and that the law is based on concepts of self-autonomy and individual responsibility — underscores this concept.

There are four areas of privacy law:

Appropriating someone's name or likeness for trade purposes – You can't take something that belongs to another person and use it for commercial gain without their permission. Their name and image belong to them. In cases of celebrity, appropriation encompasses a right to publicity as well.

Right to privacy protects one from emotional harm, while a right to publicity protects one's economic interest. One whose name has commercial value, such as a celebrity, usually can only claim a right to publicity. Often, this is a property interest that can be passed on to heirs.

Likeness can include photographs, drawings, recordings — anything that conveys the essence and likeness of an individual. Parodies, satires of celebrities, and other commentary are protected under the First Amendment. These are *transformative*, that is, they have been changed into something else to express an opinion or idea.

Trade purposes include use of a person's name in an advertisement or the use of their likeness or identity in commercial entertainment, such as a movie. Generally, the similarity of a person's name to a fictional character in a film or other entertainment vehicle is not enough to constitute an appropriation, but care is warranted.

What if a newspaper runs a picture of someone on the front page after being arrested by police? A news and information exception applies. Even though the news business must make a profit to continue publishing and broadcasting, the courts have consistently ruled that the purpose of news is different from the purpose of advertising and that photos of people in public news events are not an invasion of privacy. The greater goal in such cases is not to make a profit but to inform the public of important events in their community.

The doctrine of incidental use is another exception to the appropriation rule. This permits a fleeting or brief use of someone's name or likeness in some situations. A brief scene of a pedestrian walking down the street in a movie is not usually regarded as an appropriation.

The Booth Rule, named after actress Shirley Booth, also generally protects the media when it uses someone's name or likeness in an advertisement to promote itself if the individual is part of the news or information contained in the publication or broadcast being promoted.

Consent is a defense to an appropriation claim if certain conditions are met. Often states require that the permission be in writing. Also, consent may not be valid if there is a long delay in using the material. Generally, people have to be of legal age. And consent fails if after receiving it, the material is altered or changed. For example, you get consent to use someone's photo and then alter the image.

Intrusion upon someone's seclusion or solitude – The courts have ruled that there is no right to privacy in that which is public. But intruding on the private affairs or seclusion of an individual is actionable if it would be objectionable to a reasonable person. Taking a picture of a person in a public place is not actionable, but putting a microphone under their bed at night surely would be. No publication is required. Just the act of intruding is enough to get you into trouble.

Journalists should be especially careful when recording someone or using telephoto lenses to get information they normally would not be able to get with the naked ear or eye in public. Nor will the law protect them from illegal trespass to get a story.

Publication of private facts – It is illegal to publicize private information about a person if the information would be highly offensive to a reasonable person and the information is not of legitimate public concern. Private information would include such things as health records and bank account information or other things of an intimate nature. Courts have not been universally supportive of this law since it runs counter to basic First Amendment tenets. Nevertheless, it is recognized in a majority of jurisdictions and is gaining renewed interest as a result of the Internet and growing privacy concerns among citizens.

Of course, the information must be private. If the public is already aware of it, there can be no private interest. This also means that the information contained in public records is not private. Well-known individuals and famous people also lose some of their privacy, though not all of it. Too, those private individuals caught up in a public event lose some of their privacy. The general rule is that once a person becomes a public person he remains a public person, despite the passage of time, at least in regard to the matter that was originally published.

Publication of material that puts someone in a false light – A false light claim has similarities to libel, but again where libel is a tort against reputation, false light is a tort against peace of mind. In both situations you are making someone out to be something they are not. False light claims arise when you attribute to a person views he does not hold or actions he did not take. Thus, falsely calling someone a murderer would not only be libelous, it would also put him in a false light.

To prove a false light cause of action, the plaintiff must prove that the defendant publicized material that placed the plaintiff in a false position in the public eye, that it would be objectionable to a reasonable person, and that the defendant was at fault for doing so. The fault requirement for matters of public concern is malice.

Reporters often find themselves in trouble for false light when they distort stories for dramatic effect. Misuse of photos may also attract trouble. The guide here is to stick to the facts in stories and refrain from using photos to illustrate unrelated stories.

Consent is a defense to an action for invasion of privacy. Some states require it to be in writing, and the invasion cannot exceed the consent given. Absolute and qualified privilege may also work to defeat an invasion of privacy claim.

Corporations, businesses, and governments have no right of privacy as such.

• Open Records and Meetings •

The First Amendment, though granting citizens the right to a free press, says nothing about their right to gather the information to put in that press. In fact, nothing in the common law gives people the right to gather news or attend meetings.

To rectify the problem in part, Congress passed the Freedom of Information Act in 1966 to open up records in agencies in the executive branch of government and all the independent regulatory agencies. The Act gives any person the right to access records, including those kept electronically. The law does not cover records of Congress or the federal courts.

Nevertheless, the government added exemptions to the law. If the information falls into any categories exempted, citizens may not get the information they seek. They include national security matters covering national defense or foreign policy, housekeeping practices related to rules and practices of an agency, matters that may have been exempted by another statute, trade secrets, working papers and discovery items related to legal action, files and records that would violate personal privacy, certain law enforcement records, records relating to the supervision of financial institutions, and geological data.

Under the law, the agency must respond to citizen requests within 20 days, though someone engaged in disseminating information to the public is entitled to an expedited review if there is an urgency to inform the public about some governmental activity. Response doesn't necessarily mean you're going to get the information.

If a citizen has to file suit to get the agency to release the record and the agency loses, the agency may be assessed the cost of the citizen's legal fees and court costs. And agency personnel are personally responsible for granting or denying access, which means they can be disciplined if they arbitrarily deny access.

Agencies may charge fees for record searches and copying. Those in the news media pay no search fees and receive copies of 100 pages free. Journalists should find out which agency has the record they are looking for. Once you've determined which records you want and where they are, write a specific FOI letter to the agency requesting the information.

Journalists are often better off asking for the documents informally rather than going through the formal FOI process. See if you can find other sources for the information. In the end, the best approach is to cultivate lots of sources within the government.

In 1976, Congress extended the right to open government by passing the Government in the Sunshine Act, which opened federal meetings. The law affects about 50 federal boards, commissions, and agencies and requires them to conduct their business in the open.

Such open meeting/open record laws affect the federal government. But the states have open meeting/open records laws as well covering state agencies and records. It is important journalists become familiar with the laws in their states.

Most laws provide that in certain instances the meetings can be closed to allow board members to go into executive session. The law recognizes that in certain situations it is necessary for governmental bodies to discuss things in private, such as legal actions and personnel problems. Nevertheless, most states require that no final vote be taken on the matter behind closed doors. Most states also require that advance notice of executive sessions be given to the public. Such notice should also include what topics will be discussed or the reason for the executive session.

Journalists who believe a meeting is being closed illegally should make a formal objection and ask the board to cite the law that gives them permission to discuss the matter at hand in private. The reporter should also find out who is asking for the closed session. Finally, the reporter should call his boss. Do not resist an order to leave. Reporting on the suspect closure is better. No government official wants bad publicity.

Most states permit inspection of records by anyone, regardless of the reason. Records include both state and city government agencies, departments, boards, commissions, school districts, public utilities, and often the governor. They usually do not cover the courts or legislature. As with the federal government, state law often exempts certain records from inspection. They often mimic the federal ones. The right of inspection also usually means the right to copy.

Most state press associations have copies of their state's open meetings/open records acts. They also can be found in the state's statutes.

• Protection of Sources •

As noted in chapter five, protection of confidential sources is tricky at best. The Supreme Court has ruled that the media has no absolute privilege under the First Amendment to refuse to reveal the names of confidential sources. At best there exists a qualified privilege. So, reporters who refuse a judge's order to reveal the name of a source can be found in contempt of court. At present there is no federal shield law protecting reporters. Shield laws do exist in many states, though as noted before, their protection is limited.

Most shield laws only require those seeking the information to try to find it elsewhere first before demanding it from the reporter. Since ultimately you still may be required to divulge your source, such laws do not offer that much protection. In any case, you should be familiar with the laws of your state.

Newsroom searches also can be a problem when it comes to protecting your sources. Congress passed the Privacy Protection Act of 1980 to limit the way police and other government officials can search newsrooms and seize material from news people.

The law protects reporters' notes, photographs, and the like. It also covers government reports, documents, and other similar material the reporter gathered in pursuit of the story. Officials seeking such information generally must get a subpoena instead of a search warrant. A subpoena requires that you bring the information sought to the court instead of having police and others intrude into the newsroom on a fishing expedition to find it.

There are exceptions. A search warrant may be issued if there is reason to believe the person who has the material is committing a crime or if it's necessary to get the material to prevent death or serious bodily harm. It may also be given if there is reason to believe giving advance notice by issuing a subpoena would result in the destruction of the material or if the holder of the information has not responded to the subpoena.

• Free Press, Fair Trial •

The U.S. Constitution guarantees more than a free press. Among other rights, it also protects our right to a fair trial. Often these two fundamental liberties come in conflict with each other. What happens, for example, if wide and intense publicity about an upcoming trial makes it impossible to seat an impartial jury because citizens have already made up their minds about the guilt or innocence of the accused? On the other hand, what happens to our right to a free press if the Court prevents the Press from reporting on the matter?

Our laws don't favor one right over another. They are all important. So the Court has worked to fashion ways to protect both. The Press, too, can do things to ensure both are protected.

For example, those in the media should refrain from sensationalizing stories or suggesting the guilt or innocence of the accused before trial. The media should not focus on the defendant's character or past criminal record, the credibility of witnesses, judges or other trial participants, or anything that would inflame the public mood and make it difficult to achieve a fair trial. Unfortunately, we don't have to look far to find examples of bad press behavior.

The Court, meanwhile, has established a legal test to review the constitutionality of judges' orders that restrict the media. The test comes from the Court's 1976 decision in *Nebraska Press Association v. Stuart* (427 U.S. 539) and is referred to as the Nebraska Press Association test. In all cases, prior restraint must be the exception and not the rule. As noted before, when attempting to restrict a fundamental liberty, in this case freedom of the Press, the Court must find that there is a compelling state interest. So before such restraint is permitted, the Court has ruled that there must be a clear and present danger to the defendant's right to a fair trial.

Here is the three-part test that determines if a restrictive order is constitutional:

> **First, the trial judge must find that there is intense and pervasive publicity about the case.**
>
> **Second, the trial judge must look for, but not be able to find, another way to mitigate the effects of the publicity.**
>
> **Third, the trial judge must be able to show that his restrictive order will effectively prevent the publicity from reaching potential jurors.**

Sometimes, instead of issuing a gag order, the trial court will attempt to restrict access to a proceeding itself or to seal documents. Before making that decision, the Court must determine if the law regards the proceeding or document as presumptively open or closed. The Court must ask whether the hearing or the document has been historically or traditionally open or if keeping it open will help the judicial process. If the answer is *yes*, then the court must declare the matter to be presumptively open.

At that point, it's up to the party seeking closure to show good reason for it to be closed, and the Court must follow a five-part test before ruling on the request. The test is a result of a 1986 ruling in *Press-Enterprise v. Riverside Superior Court* (478 U.S. 1).

The test includes the following elements:

> **First, the party seeking closure must show an overriding interest that is likely to be harmed if the matter remains open.**
>
> **Second, the party seeking closure must show that there is substantial probability that the overriding interest will be harmed if the matter remains open.**
>
> **Third, the trial court must consider reasonable alternatives to closing the matter.**
>
> **Fourth, if the judge decides to close the matter, the ruling must be narrowly tailored so no more access is restricted than is necessary.**
>
> **Fifth, the trial court must support its decision with adequate findings that can be reviewed by an appellate court.**

Many judicial proceedings and documents are presumptively open. Evidentiary hearings, jury selection, sentencing hearings, bail hearings, and plea hearings are but a few. Others are presumptively closed, including grand jury proceedings and juvenile hearings.

Documents also may be presumptively open or closed. Pretrial, presentencing, post-sentencing, search warrants, information indictments, and evidence are some that are usually open. Out-of-court settlements in civil suits are routinely closed.

If a party asks the Court to close a proceeding or document of public interest that is otherwise routinely open, the reporter should make an immediate formal objection to the motion. If the reporter thinks a motion to close will be made, he should ask to talk to the judge beforehand. The reporter should tell the judge that the news organization he represents objects and would like an opportunity to argue against the motion (assuming the news organization does, in fact, object). The reporter should then ask for a recess so he can call his office and get the company's lawyer to come to court. The reporter should also ask that his objection be made part of the court record. If the judge orders the reporter to leave, the reporter should leave quietly. The reporter should then contact his editor immediately.

Lastly, when it comes to covering judicial proceedings, print reporters have a much easier time than broadcast reporters. Judges have decided that notebooks and pencils generally are less intrusive and disruptive than cameras and recording devices in the courtroom. Nevertheless, the law is slowly changing to allow such equipment in some proceedings in some states. Generally, broadcast reporters will find it easier to get their equipment into state courts than into federal courts, which have largely rejected the idea of cameras in the courtroom. Journalists should familiarize themselves with the laws of each state regarding the issue.

• Obscenity •

Obscenity law deals with a narrow class of sexually explicit expression that the Court has deemed outside the protection of the First Amendment. Consequently, it is a violation of federal law to air obscene programming. But defining just what obscenity is and what it is not has proved difficult. In 1973, the Court made its most recent attempt to define it in *Miller v. California* (413 U.S 15) and provided lower courts with a three-part test to help them determine if something was to be declared obscene. It said that material is obscene if it meets the following criteria:

> **First, an average person, applying contemporary community standards, finds the work, taken as a whole, appeals to prurient interests.** The Court has ruled that prurient interest is that which appeals to shameful or morbid interests in sex. Local standards, in most jurisdictions, mean state standards.

Second, the work depicts in a patently offensive way sexual conduct specifically defined by applicable state law. State law is to define what material or conduct is obscene.

And third, the work in question lacks serious literary, artistic, political, or scientific value. A judge or jury may be quick to determine what community standards and patently offensive material are, but the court must also look to see if a work could have value in other areas.

It is illegal to send obscenity through the mail.

Sexual material that does not rise to the level of obscenity may be considered pornographic. This class of lesser explicit material may be published.

With regard to broadcast, profanity and indecency, may, in limited instances, such as a newscast or documentary program, be transmitted, depending upon the context. Generally in over-the-air broadcasting, expletives and nudity are not allowed outside of the hours of 10 p.m. to 6 a.m. when there is a reasonable risk that children will not be watching. The Federal Communications Commission, responsible for regulating the industry, designated this time a *safe harbor* when programs not intended for children may be aired. Cable television is treated differently.

It should be noted that child pornography does not need to meet the stringent Miller test standards and is always illegal.

• Copyright and Fair Use •

If you buy a book, you own the book, but you don't own the arrangement of the words in the book. That property interest belongs to whoever holds the copyright. That means you can give the book away or burn it, but you can't reprint it without permission from the copyright holder.

Copyright law is part of the U.S. Constitution. It protects intellectual creations and falls under an area of law known as intellectual property, which also protects patents and trademarks.

Copyright does not protect facts or ideas, only the expression of those facts and ideas. The law gives the author, or holder of the copyright, the sole right to reproduce the work in whatever form he chooses. Musical works, literary works, dramatic works, motion pictures, sound recordings, choreographic works, sculptural works, photos, and the like are all protected.

News events cannot be copyrighted, but the law does protect the way a story is told. The law protects us from plagiarism — the act of taking someone's work and passing it off as your own. Under current law, any work created after January 1, 1978, is protected for the life of the creator, plus 70 years. After that, the work enters the public domain, and anyone may copy it without permission or payment to the copyright holder. Works for hire are protected for 95 years after publication. Works for hire include work that is written for a publisher. The publisher, not the author, holds the copyright.

Having said that, small amounts of a work can be copied. This is called the doctrine of fair use. The law attempts to balance the right of the author to compensation for his work while allowing the dissemination of ideas and information.

In determining fair use, the court will look to how much work is being copied and whether copying it will interfere with the author's ability to earn a profit from the work. The court also reviews the purpose of the copying. Noncommercial or nonprofit use such as teaching, criticism, opinion, scholarship and research receives wider latitude, but even here the amount and use must be limited. It must also carry the copyright notice, be spontaneous — that is, there was not time to get permission, and be brief — under 1,000 words, though that amount may be far less depending on how long the work is. Other criteria also apply.

• Telecommunications •

The law regarding telecommunications covers volumes of technical federal rules and is much too detailed to cover briefly in one book. Fortunately, for the reporter in the field covering news, it isn't necessary that we review all of them anyway. Having said that, it is nevertheless important that journalists understand a few basic points.

Of all the mass media, broadcast — particularly on-air broadcast — is regulated the most. The reason is fairly simple. In the early days of radio, to prevent broadcasters from jamming one another by transmitting on the same frequency, the government came up with a system for regulating their transmissions by assigning different frequencies to different broadcasters. Although the First Amendment prohibited government regulation of the Press on the basis of content, it could regulate the airwaves by which the broadcaster sent his signal across state lines since that belonged to the public and regulation of interstate commerce was authorized by the commerce clause of the U.S. Constitution.

Initially, in exchange for a license to transmit on the limited airwave spectrum, station owners were expected to broadcast in the public interest. Furthermore, the government sought to ensure that as many different people as possible owned the limited number of stations to increase the number of different voices in the marketplace. But as cable and the Internet developed, this public interest rationale began to erode. Instead, market forces took over and ownership rules were relaxed. Consequently, a single owner can own several TV and radio stations as well as newspapers.

When it comes to politics, the FCC imposes several important rules on broadcasters. First, the FCC requires radio and television stations and cable systems to give qualified political candidates equal opportunity to airtime. This is commonly called the *equal time rule*. There are four exemptions to this rule. Stations do not have to give equal time when candidates appear on regularly scheduled newscasts, news interview shows, documentaries that do not focus on the candidate, and spot news.

Second, stations cannot censor what a candidate says in an advertisement, but they can edit the candidate's comments in a news broadcast. Stations are not held accountable if the candidate says something libelous, though the candidate can still be sued.

Third, the equal time rule does not require that stations give or sell local or state candidates airtime. However, stations are required to make a reasonable time available to federal candidates. Stations that sell airtime to candidates must offer them the same rate it offers to its most favored advertiser.

Finally, journalists need to remember that they should not make legal decisions on their own. They should always consult a lawyer about the legal questions they face.

• Exercise •

Research *The New York Times Co. v. Sullivan* and discuss.

Appendix

SOCIETY OF PROFESSIONAL JOURNALISTS. Code of Ethics

Reprinted by permission of the Society of Professional Journalists.

PREAMBLE

Members of the Society of Professional Journalists believe that public enlightenment is the forerunner of justice and the foundation of democracy. The duty of the journalist is to further those ends by seeking truth and providing a fair and comprehensive account of events and issues. Conscientious journalists from all media and specialties strive to serve the public with thoroughness and honesty. Professional integrity is the cornerstone of a journalist's credibility. Members of the Society share a dedication to ethical behavior and adopt this code to declare the Society's principles and standards of practice.

Seek Truth and Report It

Journalists should be honest, fair, and courageous in gathering, reporting, and interpreting information.

The Journalist's Primer

Journalists should:

- Test the accuracy of information from all sources and exercise care to avoid inadvertent error. Deliberate distortion is never permissible.
- Diligently seek out subjects of news stories to give them the opportunity to respond to allegations of wrongdoing.
- Identify sources whenever feasible. The public is entitled to as much information as possible on sources' reliability.
- Always question sources' motives before promising anonymity. Clarify conditions attached to any promise made in exchange for information. Keep promises.
- Make certain that headlines, news teases and promotional material, photos, video, audio, graphics, sound bites and quotations do not misrepresent. They should not oversimplify or highlight incidents out of context.
- Never distort the content of news photos or video. Image enhancement for technical clarity is always permissible. Label montages and photo illustrations.
- Avoid misleading re-enactments or staged news events. If re-enactment is necessary to tell a story, label it.
- Avoid undercover or other surreptitious methods of gathering information except when traditional open methods will not yield information vital to the public. Use of such methods should be explained as part of the story.
- Never plagiarize.
- Tell the story of the diversity and magnitude of the human experience boldly, even when it is unpopular to do so.
- Examine their own cultural values and avoid imposing those values on others.
- Avoid stereotyping by race, gender, age, religion, ethnicity, geography, sexual orientation, disability, physical appearance, or social status.
- Support the open exchange of views, even views they find repugnant.
- Give voice to the voiceless; official and unofficial sources of information can be equally valid.
- Distinguish between advocacy and news reporting. Analysis and commentary should be labeled and not misrepresent fact or context.
- Distinguish news from advertising and shun hybrids that blur the lines between the two.
- Recognize a special obligation to ensure that the public's business is conducted in the open and that government records are open to inspection.

Minimize Harm

Ethical journalists treat sources, subjects, and colleagues as human beings deserving of respect.

Journalists should:
- Show compassion for those who may be affected adversely by news coverage. Use special sensitivity when dealing with children and inexperienced sources or subjects.
- Be sensitive when seeking or using interviews or photographs of those affected by tragedy or grief.
- Recognize that gathering and reporting information may cause harm or discomfort. Pursuit of the news is not a license for arrogance.
- Recognize that private people have a greater right to control information about themselves than do public officials and others who seek power, influence, or attention. Only an overriding public need can justify intrusion into anyone's privacy.
- Show good taste. Avoid pandering to lurid curiosity.
- Be cautious about identifying juvenile suspects or victims of sex crimes.
- Be judicious about naming criminal suspects before the formal filing of charges.
- Balance a criminal suspect's fair trial rights with the public's right to be informed.

Act Independently

Journalists should be free of obligation to any interest other than the public's right to know.

Journalists should:
- Avoid conflicts of interest, real or perceived.
- Remain free of associations and activities that may compromise integrity or damage credibility.
- Refuse gifts, favors, fees, free travel, and special treatment, and shun secondary employment, political involvement, public office, and service in community organizations if they compromise journalistic integrity.
- Disclose unavoidable conflicts.
- Be vigilant and courageous about holding those with power accountable.

- Deny favored treatment to advertisers and special interests and resist their pressure to influence news coverage.
- Be wary of sources offering information for favors or money; avoid bidding for news.

Be Accountable

Journalists are accountable to their readers, listeners, viewers, and each other.

Journalists should:
- Clarify and explain news coverage and invite dialogue with the public over journalistic conduct.
- Encourage the public to voice grievances against the news media.
- Admit mistakes and correct them promptly.
- Expose unethical practices of journalists and the news media.
- Abide by the same high standards to which they hold others.

The SPJ Code of Ethics is voluntarily embraced by thousands of journalists, regardless of place or platform, and is widely used in newsrooms and classrooms as a guide for ethical behavior. The code is intended not as a set of "rules" but as a resource for ethical decision-making. It is not — nor can it be under the First Amendment — legally enforceable.

The present version of the code was adopted by the 1996 SPJ National Convention, after months of study and debate among the Society's members. Sigma Delta Chi's first Code of Ethics was borrowed from the American Society of Newspaper Editors in 1926. In 1973, Sigma Delta Chi wrote its own code, which was revised in 1984, 1987, and 1996.

Indent for new paragraph

Insert word or letter

Separate words

Abbreviate August 30

Lower Case

b.f.
Boldface > **Boldface**

Transpose letters words or

stet
Kill correction

Story not complete at end of page.
More

Deletee

Insert apostrophe or quotes, he said

ital
Italicize > *Italicize*

wf
Wrong font > Wrong font

Insert hyphen

Eliminate paragraph

Delete woerd or letterr

Close up space

Spell out Aug. 30

capitalize letter

b,f,c.
Boldface caps > **BOLDFACE CAPS**

Join separate matter

End of story: 30 or #

Indent and/or Center

Insert period

Insert comma, he said.

rom
reset in *regular* type > regular

Insert dash

(When in doubt about the correct symbol, write out the instruction.)

Bibliography

Blundell, W. *The Art and Craft of Feature Writing: Based on the Wall Street Journal Guide*. New York: Plume, 1988.

Brady, J. *The Craft of Interviewing*. Cincinnati: Writer's Digest Publications, 1976.

Brooks, B., G. Kennedy, D. Moen, & D. Ranly. *News Reporting and Writing*. 10th ed. Boston: Bedford/St. Martin's, 2011.

Clark, T. "Bison Imagery Still Powerful." *Persimmon Hill*, Vol. 38, Issue 2 (Summer 2010): 44.

Clark, T. "Pressing On." *Oklahoma Today*, Vol. 62, Issue 4 (July-August 2012): 30.

Conrad, J. *Preface to the Nigger of Narcissus*. New York: Penguin, 1988.

DeFleur, M.L. & M. DeFleur. *Mass Communication Theories: Explaining the Origins, Processes and Effects*. Boston: Allyn and Bacon, 2010.

Dube, J. "Writing News Online." *Poynter* (March 2, 2011). www.poynter.org/how-tos/digital.../web-tips/.../writing-news-online/. Retrieved August 14, 2012.

Friend, C. "Social Contract Theory." *The Encyclopedia of Philosophy* (2004). Hamilton College. www.iep.utm.edu/soc-cont/. Retrieved September 6, 2012.

Hancock, M. *Photojournalism: What is a photojournalist?* (January 1, 1996). http://markhancock.blogspot.com/1996/01/what-is-photojournalist. html. Retrieved September 23, 2012.

King, S. *On Writing, a Memoir of the Craft*. New York: Scribner, 2000.

Knight, C. *Understanding and Appreciating the Basics of Photojournalism* (January 2010). http://photo.tutsplus.com/tutorials/understanding-and-appreciating-the-basics-of-photojournalism/. Retrieved September 23, 2012.

Landry, P. *Areopagitica by John Milton*. www.stlawrenceinstitute.org/vol14mit. html. Retrieved May 6, 2012.

Lattimore, D. & J. Windhauser. *The Editorial Process*. 2nd ed. Englewood, CO: Morton Publishing Co., 1984.

Lippmann, W. *Public Opinion*, (1922), University of Virginia. http://xroads. virginia.edu/~Hyper2/CDFinal/Lippman/cover.html. Retrieved October 3, 2012.

Orwell, G. "Politics and the English Language." *Horizon*, Vol. 13, Issue 76 (1946): 252.

Patterson, P. & L. Wilkins. *Media Ethics: Issues & Cases*. 4th ed. New York: McGraw-Hill, 2002.

Pember, D. & C. Calvert. *Mass Media Law*. 17th ed. New York: McGraw-Hill, 2011.

Pew Research Center. *Press Accuracy Rating Hits Two Decade Low* (September 13, 2009). www.people-press.org/press-accuracy-rating-hits-two-decade-low/. Retrieved October 12, 2012.

Rawls, Jr., W. "Interviewing: the crafty art." *Columbia Journalism Review*, Vol. 21, Issue 4 (November/December 1982): 46.

Rich, C. *Writing and Reporting News: A Coaching Method*. 7th ed. Boston: Wadsworth Publishing, 2013.

Rivers, W., B. McIntyre, & A. Work. *Writing Opinion: Editorials*. Ames, Iowa: Iowa State University Press, 1988.

Stovall, J. "Photojournalism." *JProf: the website for teaching journalism* (2012). http://www.jprof.com/photojn/photojn-basics.html. Retrieved September 23, 2012.

10 Top Photography Composition Rules. http://www.photographymad.com/pages/view/10-top-photography-composition-rules. Retrieved September 23, 2012.

Uzgalis, W. "John Locke," *The Stanford Encyclopedia of Philosophy*, Edward N. Zalta, editor (Fall 2012). http://plato.stanford.edu/archives/fall2012/entries/locke/. Retrieved October 10, 2012.

Ward, H. *Reporting in Depth*. Mountain View, CA: Mayfield Publishing Co., 1991.

Warnick, B. & E. Inch *Critical Thinking and Communication: The Use of Reason in Argument*. 2nd ed. New York: Macmillan Publishing Co., 1994.

White, T. *Broadcast News Writing, Reporting, and Producing*. 3rd ed. Boston: Focal Press, 2002.

Wolfe, T., editor. Forward. *The New Journalism*. New York: Harper and Row, 1973.

CPSIA information can be obtained
at www.ICGtesting.com
Printed in the USA
FSOW02n2356011215
13873FS

9 781465 211330